SEP -

Dearest Goddaughter,

It is my most earnest hope that these words are a catalyst of connection and transformation igniting a hidden and holy strength within you. That you may rise to be what you never had and live what you only once dared to dream. God is weaving something that this desperate world needs within us. Together let's be a living, breathing expression of all that it means to be a daughter of God.

Lisa

Past Praise for *Adamant*

"There is so much uncertainty in our world today. It's hard to know what or who to believe. That's why Lisa Bevere's new book, *Adamant*, is powerfully relevant. Lisa writes with confidence, poise, and grace as she leads you on a spiritual journey toward unshakable truth. Her words are timeless and timely, inviting us back to a place of sanctity, stability, and truth grounded in Christ."

Craig and Amy Groeschel, pastors of Life.Church; authors of *From This Day Forward*

"Wow! My dear friend Lisa hit a home run: 'When truth becomes fluid, we lose contact with answers larger than ourselves. Real truth is a Rock. Adamant. Indivisible. Immovable. Invincible.' In a generation and culture where truth moves with the trends, the scriptural truths Lisa shares in this book are so greatly needed."

Christine Caine, bestselling author and founder of The A21 Campaign and Propel Women

"Important. Weighty. Convicting. Lisa Bevere is relentless in her conviction to stand on and for the Truth. Her clarion voice reminds us that Truth has a Name, and it's a Name we can know. If you're longing for an unshakable place to anchor your life (and all of us are), *Adamant* will help lead you to the only unchanging Rock—Jesus. Keep this book nearby, and more often, keep its conviction-filled pages open in your hands."

Louie and Shelley Giglio, founders of Passion Conferences

"This book is profound in its wisdom, yet deeply personal. Lisa is a gifted writer and a trusted friend who will guide us to a rock-solid understanding of our true identity in Christ."

Sheila Walsh, author of *In the Middle of the Mess*

"In reading the opening pages of this bold new work, two statements resonate with my experience of the Christ and his Kingdom. 'When stripped of awe, we find ourselves clothed in confusion and comparison' and 'when truth becomes fluid, we lose contact with answers that are bigger than ourselves.' These two realities are as profound as it gets when it comes to the human condition. I am excited for what this book will stir, affirm, and ignite. In a world grasping for genuine reality, may you find wisdom for the journey, confidence of conviction, grace to be the child you truly are, and boldness to become light in the darkness for others."

Bobbie Houston, co-senior pastor of Hillsong Church

"Like a beautiful tapestry made of the most elegant fabric, *Adamant* combines Lisa Bevere's undeniable passion, vulnerability, and divine gift as wind to set each reader free. With love and understanding, Bevere takes us on a journey that will transform your mind, heal your heart, and fill your spirit with the revelation of God's perfect plan for your life."

Sarah Jakes Roberts, author of *Don't Settle for Safe*

Past Praise for *Without Rival*

"If you struggle with feelings of worthlessness or lack a sense of purpose, *Without Rival* is just what you need to silence your inner critic. God has positioned you to find contentment in the midst of any circumstance and live a life without comparison."

Pastor Steven and Holly Furtick, Elevation Church

"Lisa will help you discover how to experience the freedom and confidence that comes from knowing you are God's exclusive masterpiece—without comparison and without rival—and that you have everything you need to reach your unique God-given destiny."

Victoria Osteen, co-pastor of Lakewood Church, Houston, Texas

"I love Lisa. She is carrying such a timely word. This book is a must-read, must-believe for people. Knowing who you are and your need for others is huge! You will be strengthened as you read this, feeling the Father speak over you your true, unshakable identity."

Jenn Johnson, worship leader/songwriter with Bethel Music

"Lisa's newest book is such a treasure. It's basically the literary equivalent of God putting his hands on both sides of our face, turning our attention toward him, and then saying slowly and firmly, 'I love *you*.'"

Lisa Harper, author and Bible teacher

"Bevere's many fans will find much here to love, and she is sure to win more readers with her insights, effusive love for God, and candid explanations of personal challenges."

Publishers Weekly

Godmothers

Also by Lisa Bevere

Out of Control and Loving It!
The True Measure of a Woman
You Are Not What You Weigh
Be Angry but Don't Blow It!
Kissed the Girls and Made Them Cry
Fight Like a Girl
Nurture
Lioness Arising
Girls with Swords
Without Rival
Adamant

Godmothers

Why You Need One.
How to Be One.

LISA BEVERE

Revell

a division of Baker Publishing Group
Grand Rapids, Michigan

© 2020 by Lisa Bevere

Published by Revell
a division of Baker Publishing Group
PO Box 6287, Grand Rapids, MI 49516-6287
www.revellbooks.com

Printed in the United States of America

Library of Congress Cataloging-in-Publication Control Number: 2020004893
ISBN 978-0-8007-3685-9
ISBN 978-0-8007-3940-9 (ITPE)

The author is represented by The FEDD Agency, Inc.

20 21 22 23 24 25 26   7 6 5 4 3

Contents

One

Why You Need One

We are family!
—Sister Sledge

The cover of this book may be the first time you've seen me, but know that I carried you in my heart with every word that was typed. Why? We share the same Father. No, I didn't hijack your DNA results. We are *all* God's daughters. This simple relational statement means far more than we can possibly understand, but to start, it means we're family, and I am thrilled about it. I believe we have an intimate connection whether we ever meet in this life or the next. As daughters of God the Father, it is not a stretch to call ourselves goddaughters. And daughters need mothers who help them find their way.

Relationships matter because we are all woven together into a story. I hope you heard that. Woven means knit together, and yet a quick glance at what surrounds us reveals far too many frayed edges and torn fragments. Not only has our tapestry been compromised, it would appear that our stories are disjointed and contradictory. I believe we can be part of changing this. We can no longer afford to neglect the things that hold us together. This tale reaches beyond those who are alive in this moment to encompass all who will or ever have drawn breath. Every son and every daughter from every race and every period of time will have a part in the telling. It is not a matter of *then* and *now* or *them* and *us*; it is an eternal tale. We are the many threads that become one glorious tapestry. Let's weave something not unlike Joseph's ancient coat of many colors that declares the royalty inherent in each and every one of us.

Did you notice the wand on the cover?

No, I'm not endorsing magic; I'm advocating something deeper. I wanted to visually capture an invisible force that supersedes divination and the magic of fairy tales. The wand is but a focal point for the concept of one generation extending its blessing to the next. This blessing is the very reason godmothers should exist. They live to bless their godchildren.

Abundant life has always been far more than the abundance of things.

The godparent blessing confers fullness of life. This fullness empowers you to enjoy your life and relationships rather than imagine life is found in the collection of things. The blessing kisses our "little" and transforms it into "much." Much joy. Much hope. Much faith and much love. It is more than an edit, it is an enrichment. Abundant life has always been far more than the abundance of things (Eccles. 5:19–20).

Blessings are holy and cannot be corrupted because they come to us from our Father. The blessing of God transforms all that is visible and tangible in our lives. Blessings are meant to be shared intergenerationally. When we withhold what one generation was meant to impart to the other, there is loss on both sides. We are blessed to be a blessing to one another. And here is a beautiful truth: you can never lose what you have truly given. Like seeds, blessings multiply, and even though the seed leaves our hand, it never leaves our life. The blessing of God turns houses into homes, marriages into power unions, and children into legacy. Blessings have the power to flip crises into a catalyst for growth and transformation. The blessing can transform the very waters that the enemy meant to drown you with into a well of life for others. The blessing is when God favors your life in ways that change the enemy's narrative to work on your behalf toward your growth and benefit.

Don't imagine that I am promising that all this will make your life easy; it won't. The blessing means that all things will work together for your good (Rom. 8:28). The blessing brings rest rather than striving knowing that God is at work behind the scenes moving the right pieces into place. God's blessing expands our lives, first through our relationship with him, then in our relationships with one another, and then in resources. Connections need to be made, the blessing needs to be conferred, questions need to be answered, bridges need to be built, and some hard conversations need to be had. The wand is but the representative of what could be if all this did happen.

Even though I never birthed a daughter, I have been blessed with daughters-in-love, granddaughters, and hundreds if not thousands of daughters who call me their godmother. Perhaps, for the duration of this book, you will allow me the honor of adopting you?

I understand that I won't be your only godmother. But I am happy to be one of your many. For I do believe it will take more than one of us to bless and champion the different areas of entrustment and gifting that God has put on and in your life. Perhaps you'll consider me for the role of your scrappy, fierce Sicilian one. I'd love to point you in the direction of a more intimate connection to God the Father. It's my hope that as you turn the pages, something special happens between us and that you know you are loved, seen, celebrated, and welcome.

And if this book finds you in a later season of life, perhaps you will join me in becoming all things godmother to a generation of goddaughters.

Have you ever had a moment that is embarrassing, awful, and wonderful all at the same time? If so, you have my sympathy because I have had more than my fair share of them. Here is an example of just one of my many.

A few years ago our executive ministry staff decided to take on the challenge of transforming our approach to leadership. Each of us was invited to give ruthless, anonymous feedback on the different leaders at the ministry. The input was gathered electronically and sent to the facilitator, who compiled all the data to determine our *challenges*. Okay— that's putting it nicely. The facilitator used a different word: *constraints*.

At a later date, the group of us gathered with the facilitator. I'm going to go on record that I would have preferred a private interpretation of the results! But I've learned that leaders who want to grow have to be willing to embrace the pain of exposure and the aching nakedness of vulnerability. Here is how it went.

The facilitator began to place us in a line, situating us from the far left (least intense or aggressive) to the far right (most intense or aggressive). I was placed to the right early on. I was disheartened to watch as everyone lined up to the left of me. When it came time for my husband, John, to join the line, I breathed a sigh of relief. Finally, I'd no longer be at the end of the line. Surely, he would displace my pole position. I was shocked when the leader placed John to the left of me. Were we tied? John just smiled. Was this a joke? How could I have possibly tested higher in aggression than my alpha-male husband? Enough was enough. I protested, "There is no way I'm more aggressive than John!"

John laughed and nodded knowingly as everyone in the line turned my way. It was then I realized that even in the dead of a Colorado winter, my turtleneck sweater was a poor wardrobe choice for this type of meeting. I pulled on it. I was not just hot flashing, I was flash blushing.

The facilitator assured me there'd been no mistake. Numbers don't lie. I was the uncontested winner of the most-intense/most-aggressive spot, which immediately felt like a supreme loss.

When it was time to move on to the next result. I bolted out of my place in line, but I was too quick in breaking rank. I was told to stay where I'd been. I watched in shame as once again the entire line formed to the left of me. This time John was not placed next to me but at the opposite end of whatever spectrum this line was about to reveal.

The facilitator spoke. "This lineup represents empathy and nurture. These actions are considered the opposite of aggression—and Lisa has scored the highest in this one as well." He shook his head. "I honestly have never seen this before."

He turned toward me, seeking an explanation. My heart beat faster, but this time it was not in shame; it was in hope. I answered back, "I fight for."

Though the facilitator might not have seen this result before, I believe God has. He has a name for women who mix intense passion with empathy and nurture; they are called godmothers. And in case you are wondering if this combination is biblical, read how God describes himself in Hosea 13:8:

> Like a bear robbed of her cubs,
>   I will attack them and rip them open. (NIV)

If this description of a mama bear doesn't capture an image of feminine fierce protection of the young, I don't know what does. It is godly for mothers to fight for their children. Now let's move on to this concept of a godmother.

What comes to mind when you think of a godmother?

A fairy godmother? (Sadly, they are not a real thing.)

A mafia godmother? (Hopefully not a real thing.)

Or maybe you thought of a spiritual godmother—which desperately needs to become a *very* real thing.

Though I love to tease about it because I am half Sicilian, the godmothers I am talking about are in no way tied to the mafia. Nor can they change pumpkins into carriages or mice into horses. They are not fairies, yet they have a divine benevolent connection to the heavenly realm. Rather than a magic wand, they possess gritty grace that can be catalytic when you come in contact with it.

Godmothers are not a new idea; the concept of godparents originated in the first-century church. In those days, believers were under heavy persecution, and godparents acted as spiritual gatekeepers and guides. Godparents personally vouched for the sincerity of those who sought fellowship and sanctuary among the fledgling body of believers. One of the many ways they did this was through relational discipleship. It wasn't unusual for new converts to Christianity to be disowned by their families when they found Christ. Godparents played the role of the lost parents and were present at major life intersections such as baptisms, weddings, and funerals. It was very different than it is today when godparents simply send greeting cards on birthdays, because their communities were far more intimate. Godmothers were engaged as they walked alongside their godchildren. Each was committed to helping their daughters give expression to this glorious mystery of Christ in us. Their relationship was based on covenant rather than competition. Godmothers wanted their goddaughters to go further in their life and faith than they had traveled themselves. To this end, they lifted their daughters with what they had learned.

Though it will look different in our day, there is a desperate need for women who are more concerned with their goddaughters' destiny than their history. Godmothers believe in who their goddaughters are becoming. We need brave women who are willing to pause from their own pursuits long enough to invite some daughters along. Spiritual mamas who believe the best of their daughters while knowing they will need help to get there. Godmothers are women who are committed to growing others. This translates to speaking life, strength, and course correction to see that happen. You don't have to be old to be a godmother; you just have to be more spiritually mature.

I've been privileged to be this in one capacity or another. Whether it is online, in meetings, or through my books, there is no greater joy or honor than when a young woman calls me Mama Lisa. I remember the day my perspective shifted. I was in a meeting with our team, and they brought up my social media demographics. They asked if I knew the age of the women who follow me. I shrugged my shoulders and volunteered the age range of women close to my age. My team shared that my analytics said the largest group who followed me were women aged twenty-five to thirty-four.

I burst into tears.

Godmothers help us fill in the gaps.

It was not lost on me that my youngest son was twenty-five and my oldest was thirty-three. My team was surprised by my reaction, so I explained, "Don't you see? They don't need another speaker. They are looking for a mother." They were looking for someone to help them fill in their gaps. And we live in a time when there are quite a few gaps in desperate need of tending.

Godmothers help us fill in the gaps.

Let's talk about those gaps. When I first explored the concept of a gap or gaps, I had no idea how many words and circumstances were captured by this simple three-letter word. I found the first tier of definition from our friends at Merriam-Webster of particular interest. They define the noun *gap* as "a break in a barrier (such as a wall, hedge, or line of military defense); an assailable position."[1]

When we merge these ideas, we discover that a gap can be an area or space that renders us vulnerable to attack due to a lack of protection. The enemy of our souls loves to capitalize on and attack these assailable positions. For example, a gap in understanding becomes a misunderstanding. These breaches can quickly mire into dynamics that put relationships at risk. An information gap describes missing data that compromises our ability to make good decisions. You could call the space between the way your marriage is now and the way you hope it will be a marriage gap. The difference between the way your health is and what is optimal for you could be called a health gap. The concept of the generation gap is the breach that exists between the opinions, actions, and beliefs of the older generation and those of the younger one. I know you get the picture.

Generally speaking, a gap describes the difference or distance between the way things are and the way they should be, which is why we are so important to each other. The gaps we have in our faith, relationships, careers, marriages, and even parenting were designed to be filled by each other.

A generation of young women seems unaware that they are surrounded by mature women who'd love to open their lives and share with them what they learned the hard way. I fear they think these mothers are disinterested or oblivious. On the other hand, older women are under the mistaken impression that no one wants what they have to offer so they withdraw, become distant or combative. It's not wrong to have different viewpoints. It is so important that women in different seasons gather so we don't risk losing the richness that happens when the generations connect and share their hopes and challenges.

If the gap remains, it will leave women of all ages in an assailable position. I hear a lot of people my age and older complain about millennials and Gen Zs. Personally, I've learned a lot from my four sons, who all fall into the millennial bracket. They ask the kinds of questions that need to be answered. They push to the point of disruption and won't settle for trite answers. They want to know the *why* more than they want to know the *what*. They don't want to be told what to think; they want to learn how to think.

I believe godmothers help you discover answers to why and how. Godmothers foster a sense of purpose and community. In our day of large lives, we need intimate connections. In addition to being supportive and sharing life experiences a godmother helps you avoid future gaps and pitfalls. Openly sharing our challenges yields greater growth and a dynamic where there are more answers than questions.

In our day of large lives, we need intimate connections.

I remember when I first sensed a profound gap in my life as a young wife and mother. As a child of twice-divorced parents, I had built in some faulty protection mechanisms. I realized too late that I didn't have what I needed to build a marriage and family, and this left me vulnerable. There was a glaring gap between the way I was raised and the way I wanted to raise my children. And another gap—the size of the Grand Canyon—that represented the way my parents did marriage and the way John and I wanted to do life together. It wasn't long before I discovered that knowing what you *don't want* isn't enough to build what you *do want*. I had to be honest with myself.

I didn't know how to be a wife.

I didn't know how to be a mother.

I barely knew how to be a woman, let alone a godly one.

I felt alone because I didn't know how to find or be a true friend.

I felt frightened and isolated in my search for more than what I'd seen in ministry, marriage, motherhood, and friendship. My desperate longing for something above and beyond what I'd known or experienced only seemed to widen the gap that already existed between me and those around me. I had more questions than answers. I wondered if all the breaches in my life had made others afraid that if they got too close to me they'd fall in.

I went to church, where I was supplied with a short list of rules, most of which focused on women submitting. (Something else at which I consistently failed.) I was desperate to see a living, breathing animation of what this godly woman might look like. I certainly wasn't seeing her in the mirror. Without her in my life, all the rules only served to chain me more tightly to guilt and failure. I tried hard to be good and look more like the other pastors' wives, but I couldn't escape feeling like an outlier.

I cried out for a mentor. At the time, I didn't realize I was looking for a godmother, someone who'd notice my struggle, transform my trials, and send me along my way. I may have not known where to look, but it seemed there were none to be found. I was surrounded by young women who wrestled with the same struggles that challenged me. We all knew we were supposed to build, but no one had taken the time to show us how to use the tools or to tell us what we were building. We had saws, hammers, and lumber, but no one had a blueprint. Directionless, we settled on not causing any problems. And when problems did arise in my marriage, I hid them for fear of hearing once again that I needed to submit more. I kept cautiously moving forward, unsure of every step.

Eight years into my marriage, I found myself pregnant with our third son. John traveled full time, and as much as possible, our young family journeyed with him. On one of these trips, we'd spent over ten hours in the car traveling from our home in Apopka, Florida, to a small city in North Carolina. We arrived just in time to check into the motel that had been arranged for us. We all piled into the small room as John quickly showered and headed out the door for the service. Once he was gone, I bathed the two boys only to realize that the carpet was so dirty the bottoms of their feet were black from walking barefoot. I deposited both boys back into the tub to wash their feet. Their laughter filled the bleak room while I stripped the bedspreads off our double beds and placed them in a corner. (I am not sure that these had ever been washed!)

I lifted the boys from the tub to their bed and gave them strict instructions that there was to be no more walking on the floor. They could jump from our bed to theirs as much as they liked, but their feet could not touch the floor. They were thrilled and pretended the beds were boats and the floor was an ocean infested with alligators and sharks. It became a game. If they needed a trip to the bathroom, I was their transport.

I can still see them bouncing gleefully from bed to bed, so thrilled to be out of the confines of our car. When it was bedtime, I told them a story and sang the songs that were part of our nighttime ritual. When the time was right, I turned out the lights and sat silently in the dark, listening for the deep breaths that confirmed my boys were asleep.

John had a key to our room, but he had asked me to bolt the door behind him because the motel was in a sketchy area. Exhausted and very pregnant, I fell into a deep sleep. Hours later, John knocked softly, and I jumped out of bed, afraid he'd wake the children. As quietly as possible, John got ready, and when he climbed into bed, I asked him how the service had gone. There was a heavy sigh.

"Good. But, Lisa, it's super legalistic."

Knowing the denomination he was speaking for, I wasn't surprised. I was just getting ready to ask what he'd spoken on when John added, "The women in this church need you, so I volunteered you to do a women's meeting in the morning."

To say that my reaction was extreme would be putting it mildly. I sat up, wide awake, in bed. "Absolutely not! You can't do that to me!" I protested.

"It's done," said John with an unswerving sense of finality. "The pastor agreed, and it's already been announced."

I felt violated and utterly powerless. I told John, "Well, then you can do the meeting! I'm not doing it. I have nothing to say to those women. They'll probably stop me at the door if they notice I have double-pierced ears!"

"Don't wake the boys," John warned as he tried to make himself comfortable in the bowed double bed. "It's late. Go to sleep. I'll take the boys out to breakfast in the morning, and you can prepare your message then."

I had a sense of foreboding. "What did you preach on tonight?"

John answered. He'd preached his version of the only message I knew to preach at that time.

"How could you?" I protested. "Now I have nothing to speak on!"

I was furious. I felt robbed, dismissed, inadequate, and more than a little bit frightened by the prospect.

As a sign of protest, I abruptly turned my back to John and moved to the extreme other side of the bed. But sleep evaded me. I looked at the digital clock; it was after midnight. Soon the rhythmic breathing of my sons was punctuated by John's snoring. Everything about the small room felt unfamiliar: the smells, the lumpy pillow, the scratchy sheets, and the harsh fluorescent light peeping through the breach in the blackout curtains. I wished for home and my own bed.

My mind raced. What could I possibly say to a gathering of church women who couldn't even wear pants? I wasn't a minister. I was a mother. I cradled the baby in my womb, comforted by his gentle movements. I watched as the hours passed on the digital clock—1:00 a.m., 2:00 a.m., 3:00 a.m.—and still sleep evaded me.

At some point I must have drifted off because the next thing I knew was John standing over me with his hand on my arm. I was disoriented by the unfamiliar surroundings and the harsh realization that the night before had not been a nightmare. In the morning light, it was a looming reality.

"I wanted to let you sleep as late as possible," John volunteered.

I looked at the clock and flew into a panic. The meeting I was tricked into speaking at would begin in a few short hours, and I still had to shower and prepare some sort of message.

All I wanted was coffee . . . and ice cream for breakfast.

I'm not sure I ate that morning.

I kissed and hugged my sleepy boys, then the three of them were gone and I was alone—if very pregnant counts as alone. I showered and dressed in record time, desperate to hear from God.

First on my agenda was a massive change in attitude. I didn't want to go into the meeting mad at my husband and a pastor I hadn't met. I hate having my choices taken away, but I knew my frustration went deeper. I was angry older women hadn't prepared me for this. I was sure someone had seen my gaps but refused to help close them. I imagined them happy that I had gaps. But if I was honest, my angst reached even further than them.

I was angry and frustrated with God!

Getting up in front of strangers was no small thing. But even worse, how could I possibly be expected to give what I didn't have? How could I possibly help them with what they needed when I didn't have what I needed? I felt overwhelmed and turned all the protests swirling in my head into a prayer. Kneeling atop the bed, I closed my eyes and lifted my voice:

Father,

Before I was married, you asked me to minister to women. I said I would if you sent me a mentor. Well, it's been more than eight years and you haven't sent anyone. My life is surrounded by males, not females. God, I don't like women! They don't say what they mean or mean what they say. I like guys better because I always know where I stand with them. This isn't fair. I've been tricked into doing this meeting by John. I didn't ask to do this service.

I rambled on until I ran out of protests. Finally, I was quiet. What I heard next surprised me with its simple directness.

"Lisa, I like women."

Fair enough.

I should have already known this, but for some reason this revelation reverberated through my entire being, bringing my scattered thoughts to full attention. I was silenced and my complaints arrested. For the first time, I realized my anti-female sentiments were insulting to all his daughters and my sisters. In that moment, I knew the mandate that he had whispered into my heart nearly a decade earlier was about to begin. I dreaded it. I felt completely ill-equipped for it, but I could no longer avoid it. Inwardly, I surrendered, and I nodded a yes as I whispered, "But . . . you never sent me a mentor."

I don't know what I expected to hear, perhaps "Sorry"? But what I heard was, "Lisa, for you there will be no mentor."

This answer felt so sad, so final. Wasn't I worthy of a mentor? I felt a profound sense of loss. I could not imagine I'd be able to do anything but fail. I buried my face in the pillow and cried. I felt doomed to loneliness. But before I went too far down that path, the Holy Spirit redirected my focus.

In my mind's eye, I saw a massive chain descending from the sky. This chain was strong, but it wasn't a chain that imprisoned; its links adorned. Each link was perfectly formed and glittered with the warmth and brilliance of gold. I looked up but couldn't perceive where the chain began. I did notice where it ended. It stopped abruptly and was followed by an empty space, where a link appeared to be missing. After this gap, another length of chain began. This chain hung in midair, suspended but isolated from the last link in the first long chain. This void became my focus. As I wondered why there was a disconnect, in my spirit I heard, "There has been a break from one generation of women to the next."

I sensed I was seeing in my spirit the very thing I so keenly sensed the loss of in my life. I heard, "I don't want a mentoring of pride. I want a mentoring of brokenness. I want mothers. Be that woman."

The idea of me ever being that woman was laughable.

"I don't know how to be that woman," I protested.

"Yes, you do," he countered. "Everything you wish another woman would have been to you these last eight years, you begin to be."

As though to comfort me, the Holy Spirit whispered, "Lisa, write it backward. Then be what you needed."

Maybe that would work.

My heavenly Father asked me to be the woman I'd looked for.

I took up pen and paper and began to imagine her. As I caught glimpses, I wrote. What did I hope she'd see when she looked at me? How would she treat me? What did I need from her?

I hoped she'd see promise and potential in me yet help me to grow beyond my fearful weaknesses. She would protect, nourish, and nurture what was on my life. She would open the pages of her own stories so I could learn from her struggles. She'd teach me to laugh at my future even as I cried in the moment. She would be there for me, but rather than being *on my side* (for, surely, I can be wrong), she would be *by my side*. She'd be caring rather than controlling. She'd tell me truth in ways I could hear it. She'd open the treasury of her life and teach me the wisdom of God's seasons and the rhythm of his timing.

> She'd teach me to laugh at my future even as I cried in the moment.

I was thirty at the time, half the age I am now. I remember I was afraid those openings would allow the wind to blow into places I wasn't ready to explore. The breaches exposed portions of my life I didn't feel equipped to address. As time passed, I learned it is better to acknowledge our gaps than to excuse, deny, or avoid them. I've learned to embrace the light of revelation they bring into my life.

For three decades now, I've ministered to women. I've spoken at conferences around the globe and read countless letters, emails, and social media posts. I've had the honor of discipling women up close and from afar. It matters not whether I am in America, Egypt, Iraq, or Europe, women are hungry for more. They realize there is an aching need for deeper multi-generational connections. Both the young and the not-so-young mourn the gap but don't always know viable ways to bridge or fill it.

For far too many spiritual mothers and daughters, there is a yawning gap that has left both ends of the age spectrum at risk. Not long ago, I was speaking at a conference with a younger woman who is a powerful minister. I invited her up to my room for coffee. At first, she declined. Then she decided to accept and she joined me. She apologized for avoiding me earlier and explained that she'd already been betrayed and hurt by some older women. I empathized and explained that was not who I wanted to be in her life.

Navigating these disconnects requires courage because the loss of connection threatens all. I haven't always done this well, but I am committed to building differently in the future. How about we let go of the past patterns and change this? As God-related women, it's time to push aside the hurt and move forward, arm in arm with one another.

Recently, a young woman reached out to me and shared that she wanted to step away from the safe and settled places in her life, but she was afraid. I've been in that place of fear and have journeyed the road she is planning to tread. As a godmother, I assured her, "Scary is God's new fun." Lovely one, if you were meant for safety and ease, you would have been born in another time period. If you are hoping to live small, put this book down now for there is no reason to engage a godmother. But if you are looking to grow, by all means, grab one!

Sometimes the scariest thing is admitting that there is a gap that you don't know how to fill. Is it a challenge in your marriage? The season of life you're in? Raising your children? Finding your purpose? Where do you need to grow?

No matter what it is, guess what? You were not made to fill all these gaps yourself. You were made for a relationship with a godmother: a woman who worships the one true God and positions others both spiritually and practically to navigate their crucial and catastrophic seasons in life. She will help you find meaning and humor in the mundane. A godmother mourns the losses and celebrates the victories of her goddaughters. She lives with the understanding that being a mother in *any* capacity is the greatest challenge and honor life can bestow. She is there when you need her, yet she has limits

Sometimes the scariest thing is admitting that there is a gap that you don't know how to fill.

and understands God is the ultimate source of life. More than just watching you, she watches over you. She leans in when others have left and loves when others aren't looking. It is my prayer that you will recognize the seeds of an extraordinary life within the ordinary. That what you have now will reveal itself as all that you need to simply begin. By simply opening this book, you've invited growth, and growth always involves a good dose of risk. There will be danger—not to who God created you to be but to the old ways and patterns you've lived.

It is my earnest prayer that as you move through this book and not only ponder but do the very things these words awaken in you, you will find the courage to step into your story. As you look for that godmother to do life with, let my words accompany you and be assured that God the Father is for you. He is ultimately the One who fills every gap.

Godmother Conversation Starters

Do any gaps come to mind? Don't be afraid to answer this because these are the areas of your potential *growth*.

Have you been asking the right questions of the right people to discover the *answers* you need? Or have you simply been speaking to people in your same season of life who have the same challenges?

Are you willing to remove some of your current limits and dream about future *possibilities*?

Two

Begin with What You Know

It may be hard for an egg to turn into a bird: it would be a jolly sight harder for it to learn to fly while remaining an egg. We are like eggs at present. And you cannot go on indefinitely being just an ordinary, decent egg. We must be hatched or go bad.

—C. S. Lewis

Recently, I met a goddaughter.

This rendezvous was completely unexpected. We were away with a group of friends, celebrating John's sixtieth birthday, when I had a chance to join a friend for a free facial. After nearly two continuous weeks on the road, I was thrilled by this generous offer and my face was in desperate need. We were ushered into the spa locker area, where we peeled off our workout clothes to wrap ourselves in soft heated robes and exchanged our shoes for slippers. Dana headed for the steam room. Steam is never a good option with my crazy hair, so I headed out to the relaxation area.

As I entered a spacious room, I was greeted by a wall of glass that framed a pristine mountainscape. Irresistibly drawn, I shuffled closer to the window. After the long winter, I wanted to feel the sunlight on my face. As I approached, I noticed two women whispering among themselves in the high-back chairs closest to the window. I respectfully retreated to the array of herbal teas, flavored water, and fruit. Taking a seat against the far wall, I nibbled on fresh berries while I awaited my spa turn. When the berries were gone, I saw a display of magazines on the circular table and decided to leaf through a few. I watched as a young woman entered the room. She too was utterly captivated by the view of the mountains. I understood. I was about to settle back down in my chair when she turned and saw me.

I'm sure what I am about to describe has happened to you before. You know someone recognizes you, but you don't recognize them. It's an awkward moment. My mind raced through my memory files looking for clues that would tell me how we knew one another. She looked to be the age of my sons and daughters-in-love. Was she one of their friends? I smiled. That was when she revealed the book she held tightly in the curve of her arm. It was a copy of *Without Rival*. I moved in closer, hugged her, and invited her to sit with me.

This beautiful young woman was in a season of so many new beginnings. She was newly married, and they'd just moved away from friends and family. They were on a great adventure to discover all that God had for them both. Knowing she was in the midst of a lot of transition, a sweet friend of hers had entered her name into a contest to win a trio of my books. And the wonder of it all was that by the convergence of a lot of unlikely chances, we were now engaged in conversation in a spa. Her eyes sparkled with tears as she shared what the book had already meant to her. She opened the pages and showed me her highlighting. It had been only a few days since she'd started the book, but she was already deep into it. I listened. It was so evident that she loved God, loved the church, loved his Word. She desperately wanted to please God and yet found herself frozen by confusion. She wasn't sure if she was hearing God's voice, her own, or, even worse, the voice of the enemy.

I assured her that the enemy of our souls has long been known to do his best to turn our good intentions against us by whispering seeds of doubt and lying innuendos. It was obvious to me that this young couple's lives were brimming with potential. No wonder the enemy was working overtime to try to stop them in their tracks. She summed up all her questions and fears with one phrase: "I'm afraid I will *miss God.*"

I only wish this was the first time I'd heard this fear. I find it to be one of the most common concerns among the most selfless and tender Christians. And, of course, everyone who claims to be a follower of Christ should make it their goal to follow where he leads rather than go their own way.

On the surface, this fear of "missing God" sounds noble, but time has taught me that the enemy pounces on it, then uses it to entrap people. It is his ploy to make everything about our performance rather than our trust in God's grace. *It changes the focus to our ability to follow rather than his ability to lead.* This makes our Christian walk fear-driven rather than love- and faith-based. The enemy of our souls knows that every daughter of God wants to please her Father. Satan perverts our godly desire to follow God's leading by questioning every move we make until confusion traps us in inaction. Listen, Jesus is not trying to trick you. He would not tell us to follow if it was impossible. His ways are simple, but they are not easy.

The enemy knows that one way to stop the purehearted is to freeze them with the fear of making a wrong move. He knows that the immobilized cannot follow. I want you to hear me, lovely goddaughter: I actually believe that if your heart is pure, it is impossible to miss God. Why do I think this?

He is just too big of a target. Lovely one, answer me this:

Where can you aim and not come in contact with him?

Where can you reach and not touch something that declares his existence?

Where can you look and not see the fingerprints of his majesty?

Look up and you discover his wonder in the stars.

Look down and see his glory in a flower.

The mountains' heights remind us that he is our Rock of refuge.

The ocean's roar declares his undeniable might.

The wind awakens our souls to his unseen presence as it whispers, "There is more."

We are promised that if we will but seek him with all our heart, he will be found by us. And if this knowledge doesn't inspire you, there is even more good news. You, lovely goddaughter, are surrounded. Never again imagine there is a place or circumstance where you are alone. In *Letters to Malcolm*, C. S. Lewis highlights this truth: "We may ignore, but we can nowhere evade, the presence of God. The world is crowded with him. He walks everywhere incognito."[1]

> *It is impossible to miss God. He is just too big of a target.*

Who else but the Spirit of God is omnipresent? This literally means present in all places at all times. No moment or place exists without his presence; there has never been a space void of him, not in your past, present, or future.

Try as they might, your parents weren't capable of this. Your friends can't be this to you, and if your husband is like mine, he isn't omnipresent even when he is present. But none of this is true of the Holy Spirit. The Spirit of the Most High God surrounds us even as we are indwelled. If you open the eyes of your understanding, you will see the Spirit's presence on the pages of your Bible. God's Holy Spirit never contradicts God's Holy Word, but the expression of the Living Word is not limited to ink on sheets of paper or the data on an electronic device. If this is true, how did the early saints survive? Very few could read, and the first Bible wasn't printed until 1454. Just as the Spirit is heard in the spoken Scriptures, his imprint is on everything the Word (Jesus) created. We can thank him for all that we see, the food we eat, the flowers we smell, the materials we construct our homes with, the sounds we hear, and every living creature that draws breath. Each of us bears the mark of the Creator. (I am calling foul on snakes, scorpions, and spiders!)

Goddaughter, would the one who sent his only begotten Son to rescue you watch for your failure or look for an excuse to abandon you? God forbid the thought! Lovely one, fear not, you are his. Redeemed, washed, beloved, and righteous in his sight.

As his, is there anywhere you can go that our Father is not present? King David pondered this question and reflected on the awe of God's intimate presence in Psalm 139:

> You hem me in, behind and before,
> and lay your hand upon me.
> Such knowledge is too wonderful for me;
> it is high; I cannot attain it. (vv. 5–6)

David was saying . . . I can't even realize, grasp, or achieve this. To be hemmed in is yet another way of saying surrounded. I believe this is both spatial as well as dimensional. God is in our past and future. Our Father is more than an observer; he is in touch with us. David described this as God's hand upon his life. God is involved with us. He is that hand of comfort as well as the one that takes us by the hand to lead us. His hand is upon our head in blessing. He is the hand that holds us back from danger. When God puts his hand on something, it confers blessing and an awareness of his anointing. David called this awareness too wonderful and too high to attain. It is beyond our reach to comprehend and far beyond our ability to earn.

And just to be sure that none of the richness and beauty of this was lost in translation, I'm including these verses from the Message paraphrase as well:

> I look behind me and you're there,
> then up ahead and you're there, too—
> your reassuring presence, coming and going.
> This is too much, too wonderful—
> I can't take it all in! (Ps. 139:5–6 MSG)

Are you hearing this?

An awareness of God is meant to overwhelm us.

In this moment, he is there with you, even as he is here with me. God's presence doesn't require a church building, a song, or a sermon. His children are the focus of his presence. *Emmanuel* means "God with us," and this one word is our reassurance of his presence.

In the Old Testament, the anointing of God's presence rested predominantly on the prophet, priest, and king. The cloud by day and the pillar of fire by night set the people of Israel apart as his own. But now, his presence is for us as well! Our welcome was proclaimed with the birth of Jesus, our Emmanuel:

> And the angel said to them, "Fear not, for behold, I bring you good news of great joy that will be *for all the people*." (Luke 2:10)

In essence, the angel said, "Don't be afraid. Open your heart and eyes. I have an announcement of good news; everyone is included, so dare to let your hearts overflow with joy!"

When my children were little, they'd pull a blanket over their heads and imagine they'd disappeared from our sight. God is not blind to our plight just because we can't see him. In the garden of Eden, Adam and Eve did the same thing.

> And they heard the sound of the Lord God walking in the garden in the cool of the day, and the man and his wife hid themselves from the presence of the Lord God among the trees of the garden. (Gen. 3:8)

When you think about it, this is at once tragic and funny. They thought they could hide from the Creator behind the trees he'd created. But it is just as silly for us to imagine that there is a place in our lives that is hidden from his presence. The good news is that just as there is *no place* to hide, we have *no reason* to hide.

We have this assurance:

> And no creature is hidden from his sight, but all are naked and exposed to the eyes of him to whom we must give account. (Heb. 4:13)

The fact that we are all naked and exposed is the very reason we needed a High Priest who understood the pain of being naked and exposed. The writer of Hebrews continues,

> Since then we have a great high priest who has passed through the heavens, Jesus, the Son of God, let us hold fast our confession. For we do not have a high priest who is unable to sympathize with our weaknesses, but one who in every respect has been tempted as we are, yet without sin. (Heb. 4:14–15)

Since we have a High Priest who understands that our struggle is real, we can hold fast in faith. And because we believe that the triumph of his victory is greater than the struggle of our reality, we draw near to God without fearing his rejection.

> Let us then with confidence draw near to the throne of grace, that we may receive mercy and find grace to help in time of need. (Heb. 4:16)

He knows what we've done just as God knew what needed to be done to redeem us. Stripped of all clothing, Jesus took our sin on the barren tree of the cross to take on the shame of our nakedness and cover us with his eternal righteousness.

Precious goddaughter, the enemy of your soul does not want you to know this. He wants you to cling to images of an angry, removed God who watches you like a critic on the sidelines of your life, arms crossed, waiting for you to fail. And when you fail—because you will fail, for none of us fails to fail—he hopes you will imagine that your Father steps away. He doesn't want you to realize that when you fall or falter, your Father moves closer. He hopes you will think that God turned his back on you or worse . . . that he gives up on you and leaves. The enemy pushes this line

> *We believe that the triumph of his victory is greater than the struggle of our reality.*

of deception, hoping that you will respond to an imagined abandonment by turning your back on God.

Hear me, goddaughter:

Our heavenly Father is not like that.

He is all good. He is unlike even the best father any of us has known.

His goodness is beyond our comprehension.

David continues to paint the vastness of God's personal connection with us in the following verses:

> Where shall I go from your Spirit?
>   Or where shall I flee from your presence?
> If I ascend to heaven, you are there!
>   If I make my bed in Sheol, you are there! (Ps. 139:7–8)

Sheol is the realm of shadow and death. Yet there is no shadow that can separate you from his presence. Death cannot divide you from the King of Light. The Message says it this way:

> Is there anyplace I can go to avoid your Spirit?
>   to be out of your sight?

If I climb to the sky, you're there!
If I go underground, you're there! (Ps. 139:7–8)

There is no height you can climb that is beyond his reach or rescue. No pit you can dig that is so deep he cannot draw you out. He is the God of the heavens, and yet the dark realms of the underworld tremble when his name is whispered.

Daughter, stop worrying . . . it's exhausting.

Stop fearing that you've missed God; you haven't.

Stop thinking you haven't done enough, because you actually can't.

> Stop thinking you haven't done enough, because you actually can't.

Stop hiding because shame said you weren't enough.

We are not the answer.

It is Jesus who is more than enough.

You are surrounded; you might as well throw your arms up in the air and just surrender to his love and truth.

He is with you, near you, loving you.

Close your eyes and whisper his name:

Jesus.

At this name and in this moment, any distance you've imagined has been spanned, every breach closed, and every paralyzing fear has taken flight.

Why are we trying so hard *to be good*? It's impossible.

We can only do good, and any good thing we have, he has given us.

Invite the light of his love to expose the shadowed lies of the evil one.

What if you mess up? Who hasn't? What if you've spent the last week, month, year, or decade frozen in fear? Goddaughter, you possess a greater power than any imaginary magic wand. It is the power of choice. You have the right to decide that tomorrow will be different! It is time to break the bonds of the lie and move forward.

Hear this:

> The steadfast love of the LORD never ceases;
>   his mercies never come to an end;
> they are new every morning;
>   great is your faithfulness. (Lam. 3:22–23)

His love *never* ends.

His mercy *never* runs out or ceases to exist.

Why? It is utterly inexhaustible. The love and mercy he personally *feels for you* and *is for you* renews *every* morning.

Each day is a reset. When you woke this morning, his heart leapt with love and mercy toward you. Not once did he think, *She was such a disappointment yesterday. I hope she doesn't mess up again today.* You may think that or your parents may have said that, but never your Father.

He watched over you as you slept and rejoiced when you woke. I wonder if he is thinking, *I can't wait to surprise her with my love; yesterday is gone and today is a fresh start.*

In the words of *Anne of Green Gables*, "Tomorrow is always fresh, with no mistakes in it yet."[2]

The enemy of your soul does not want you to believe this. He wants you to carry any balance of blame forward so he can shroud you in the shadow of residual shame. He wants you crushed under the weight of every mistake and condemned for every sin-filled moment of a thousand yesterdays.

He wants today stripped of its strength so that tomorrow's hope is aborted. He mocks any attempt you make with declarations of his own: "You failed yesterday, and you will fail again today. Why try? Don't you see your pattern?"

Yes, when we look back, we will always discover a pattern, but when we lift our hearts to God, we discover a path. The enemy wants you to look back so that you will go back. Don't do it. Embrace God's path of love and mercy. The enemy is relentless in his attempts to tear aside the love and mercy that surrounds you. Here is another layer of wonder: the God who is hard to miss, who surrounds you, is having you followed!

SURROUNDED AND FOLLOWED

> Surely goodness and mercy shall follow me
>> all the days of my life,
> and I shall dwell in the house of the LORD forever.
>> (Ps. 23:6)

He has commissioned his goodness and mercy to follow us until we find our forever home! We can't miss him because we are surrounded, and he has our back!

It'd be a grave mistake to imagine that it is *our* goodness and mercy that follow us. I probably don't need to tell you this, but it is not the goodness and mercy of our brothers and sisters that follow us. We may bask in the goodness and mercy of our friends on some days, but only God shadows us on all our days! God alone is pure goodness and mercy. The word *follow* implies there is movement. It's difficult to follow someone who isn't moving. Of course, even if

Yes, when we look back, we will always discover a pattern, but when we lift our hearts to God, we discover a path.

we stand frozen by fear or indecision, his mercy and goodness remain; but wouldn't it be better for us to move so others can experience the wonder of their wake? Peter made a bold move that could be perceived as a mess-up.

> And Peter answered him, "Lord, if it is you, command me to come to you on the water." He said, "Come." So Peter got out of the boat and walked on the water and came to Jesus. But when he saw the wind, he was afraid, and beginning to sink he cried out, "Lord, save me." (Matt. 14:28–30)

I am glad Peter stepped out of the boat without any prequalifiers. I'm glad he simply said, "Jesus, if it is you, then I am out of the boat." Peter didn't doubt until he saw what the wind was capable of. Nowadays, this interaction might sound like, "Jesus, if it is you and you can guarantee that I am not going to sink or look like an idiot in front of my friends, then I will come." I think Jesus would say, "No, my friend, just stay where you are." Sometimes you have to risk it all first to walk on water. Peter sank, but he also was the only disciple who ever walked on water.

What do you need to risk? What are you afraid of? What horrible thing have you done that he cannot use as an opportunity for your instruction? Are you trying to hide it? We already discussed how silly it is to imagine we can hide anything from the One who sees everything.

It is too much for you to carry; lay it now before him as an offering. Is it a sin, misstep, or mistake that the enemy or religion has told you is beyond God's grace and mercy?

Even if people cannot forgive you . . . he has. Receive it.

Goddaughters, it's time to step out of the boat and be brave. It's time to stop making excuses or futilely imagining we can pay for our sins. Let's do an about-face and turn to God. This about-face is repentance.

The gift of repentance transforms the ugliest of our actions, seasons, places, and portions of life into spaces of hope for others. As we yield them to our Lord, he turns them around for his glory.

Over the course of time, every memory of sin that the enemy flashed across my mind hoping to cause me to cringe and cower has been redeemed without a trace of shame. Every time the serpent whispered, "You can't say that because you didn't live that," the lie was exposed, and I found my voice and used it to lift others. I dare you to find your voice and do the same.

His mercy, love, and nearness are gracious gifts meant to be treasured and not misused. Precious things should not be treated as though they were common. This revelation comes with a warning:

> What shall we say then? Are we to continue in sin that grace may abound? By no means! How can we who died to sin still live in it? (Rom. 6:1–2)

Even though his love and forgiveness are inexhaustible, don't imagine they are cheap. We live in a world where the laws of economics tell us that the greater the supply, the cheaper the cost and the greater the demand, the greater the cost to the consumers. Thankfully, the kingdom of God runs on a completely different economic system from ours. The greater the demand (need), the lower the cost to the consumers (us) and the greater the expense to the provider. God gave his only begotten Son to redeem those trapped in darkness whom sin had rendered worthless in the eyes of this world.

> Do you not know that all of us who have been baptized into Christ Jesus were baptized into his death? (Rom. 6:3)

He surrendered his all for us; therefore, we can do no less than surrender our all to him. He died for us, and we enter into his work of death that leads to life.

Therefore, these great and glorious promises are made to those who are in Christ . . . the goddaughters and godsons. These words are written to the willing rather than to the willful. As long as we are goddaughters with humble, surrendered, and teachable hearts, he causes all things (the good, the bad, the stupid, the sinful, the dirty, and the very ugly) to work together for good.

CHRIST OUR ADVOCATE

> My little children, I am writing these things to you so that you may not sin. But if anyone does sin, we have an advocate with the Father, Jesus Christ the righteous. He is the propitiation for our sins, and not for ours only but also for the sins of the whole world. (1 John 2:1–2)

The sins of the world have been covered. Thank God that heaven knew we would need this. The hope is that we would *not* sin but when we *do*, there is a provision. This is probably not going to surprise you.

I sin.

You sin.

We sin.

I am not trying to be flippant about sin. Sin is far too destructive and dangerous to treat it casually. I just want to make the point that outside of Christ none are sinless.

The hope is that as we know and grow, we will sin less.

I've said this before, but it bears repeating. Making a mistake does not make you a mistake, and if you think it does, then you are mistaken. We who have made and will make mistakes are in good company. The only failure that is certain is the failure of what was left undone.

Making a mistake does not make you a mistake, and if you think it does, then you are mistaken.

Abraham, Sarah, Moses, King David, and King Solomon are but a sampling of the heroes of faith from the Old Testament who sinned or made horrific mistakes. When we look to the New Testament, we have the elite apostles Paul, Peter, and Thomas messing up. And yet they all were in the plan of God even *after* messing up. Why would any of us imagine it would be different for us? Don't imagine, lovely one, that you have messed up the plan of God for your life; you are not that powerful.

There is but one who is sinless and but one who has never strayed . . . Jesus. And whenever you turn back to him (repent), there is a reset. This means the mess-up isn't the end of the story.

So, take a deep breath, goddaughter, and begin with the assurance of the following:

He is near.

You can't miss God . . . he is everywhere.

You are surrounded . . . his hand is upon you.

You are being followed . . . he's got your back.

If you can't miss, then you don't have to be stressed.

Set your heart on him, and move forward in confidence.

46

Godmother Conversation Starters

What are the areas of life where you have been frozen by the fear of missing God?

How do you feel about being surrounded and followed?

What is one action you can take now to begin moving forward?

☆ *Three* ☆

Ask for What You Need

Spiritual maturity is not knowing what to do with your whole life, but just knowing what to do next.

—*Henri Nouwen*

As long as your heart is set on pilgrimage, don't be afraid to tell your feet to just keep walking. It is easier for God to turn you when you are moving than when you freeze. Dare to take a step. Or in the words of Henrietta Mears, "It is difficult to steer a parked car, so get moving."[1]

It is easy for me to say this with complete confidence because I have experienced God's faithfulness for nearly forty years. And yet I understand because I distinctly remember having this same struggle in my season of new beginnings.

I was fresh out of college, newly married, in a new city, with no job experience and no connections. I took a bookkeeping position in the accounting department in a church. I was diligent but utterly miserable. It was an incredibly tense atmosphere that tied my stomach in knots. Conversations were rare with all of us counting money, but when anyone did talk, it leaned toward gossip. As much as possible, I kept my head down and my mouth shut. But even so, I couldn't avoid the slights about my past, my clothes, and even my marriage. After work, I'd run into our apartment, almost knocking John over when he tried to hug me, in a mad dash to use the bathroom.

Baffled, John would ask, "Why don't you use the restrooms at work?"

"I can't," I would protest from behind the closed door. "If you walk out of the room, everyone talks bad about you."

I'd learned the hard way that there was mean—and then there was church-lady mean. I wasn't willing to take any more chances than I had to.

Finally, John had enough. "Lisa, you need to get another job. You hate it, and I doubt that bookkeeping is a lifelong career for you."

At the time, John was working as an engineer, and the little bit of money that I earned was just buffer income.

But I was afraid to quit. I had lost my very first job out of college. Fired straight out of the starting gate. I was afraid I'd disappoint God if I left a job that was in any way related to the ministry. Afraid of what the people at work might think and say. Afraid I wouldn't be able to get another job and afraid I'd have to go back to waitressing. Afraid that I'd be a constant financial drain on our marriage and never make any meaningful financial contribution to our household. I was afraid to leave and afraid to stay. Afraid was my normal.

So many fears had me utterly frozen.

I could have just listened to John and quit. I could have pulled the submission card and hid behind John and announced with full confidence, "My husband doesn't want me working here anymore so I'm quitting."

They might even have been impressed by how submissive I'd become. But it would not have been an honest or even an obedient approach. John would have served as a shield for me to hide behind. Ultimately, I, not John, would have to live with the consequences of my choices.

In pursuit of some direction, I set some time aside that weekend to pray and hear from God. I've learned that God has no problem speaking to us through the Scriptures, and I needed a promise to carry me forward whether I stayed or moved on to another position. Sitting cross-legged on our bed with my Bible in my lap, I closed my eyes and prayed. I began by spilling out everything: my fears, confusion, frustration, and inadequacies, and a prevailing sense of hopelessness.

I asked the Holy Spirit to lead me, quieted my soul, and listened. Almost immediately in my spirit, I distinctly heard both a Bible chapter and verse, but I pushed back. I was afraid to look up the verse because it was from an Old Testament weeping prophet that I avoided reading. I questioned myself. Was I making this up? Did this book in the Bible even have that many chapters? Trembling, I opened my Bible to check out how many chapters the book in question had. There were more than fifty. I took a deep breath and opened my Bible to the book of Jeremiah, chapter 29, verse 11, and this is what I found:

> "For I know the plans I have for you," declares the LORD, "plans to prosper you and not to harm you, plans to give you hope and a future." (NIV)

Immediate tears.

You probably knew what I was going to find, but I did not. In that moment, these verses became a personal assurance that I was seen, my prayers were heard, and my fears were understood.

Our Father was saying *then to me* what I believe he is speaking *now* to you, "Baby girl, I have a plan. Don't be afraid. It is a plan for good and not harm. This plan is not limited to you or your now. It's bigger than a job. My plans extend to include your future and hopes you don't even know how to put into words yet. I've got this."

That's all I had, but it was more than enough. God had spoken. What a relief. I didn't have to figure everything out. And guess what? Neither do you. Hear me, frozen goddaughter: the God you can't miss hasn't missed a thing.

He knows the pain. He knows the discouragement. He knows how you've failed. He knows how others have failed you. He knows the fears that have frozen you. He's heard their whispers. He's heard the plans they made for you.

The God you can't miss hasn't missed a thing.

But none of that matters. Their words are like dust that is blown away by the wind. It is the Word of the Lord that will prevail and endure forever.

He will blow their vain words away like chaff as he establishes *his plan*. He laughs at the treachery of the enemy and uses what was meant to stop you as obstacles that prepare you. His plan will prosper your soul, bless the work of your hands, and cause the legacy of your life to thrive. There is laughter in your future. Dare to hope because God's plan is so much greater.

His plan uses the enemy's plan for your benefit.

Rather than cowering, allow every hardship you encounter to work a new strength within you. Watch for the plot twist, because what others meant for evil, God will turn around for your good.

Lovely one, get up, lift your head, and begin again. It's not the end of the story. There is a future hope for you. If you don't see it in your lifetime, it doesn't matter. His plans are not limited to our time in this temporal realm. Have you forgotten that you are a daughter of eternity?

God is near, he's got your back, and he has a plan.

THERE IS A PLAN

When my four sons were little, John traveled *a lot*. This meant that until my boys got older they had to go on *a lot* of errands with me. Which they hated *a lot*. I found the best approach to these outings was to surprise them and withhold explanations until we were already in the car. At any given moment, I might discover we were low on groceries and yell out, "Hey, guys, everyone in the car!"

That was when the collective protests began.

"Are we doing errands?"

"I hate shopping!"

"How many stores are we going to?"

"How long will we be gone?"

"Are we going to the doctor's?"

"Will I get a shot?"

"Will we eat?"

"Can I stay home?"

I had a plan. It was to do them good and not harm. It usually involved school supplies, clothing, or food for their future.

I could only answer them according to what I knew, and most of the time I was unsure. If I said we'd be gone an hour and the shopping escapade ended up taking three hours, then I was in trouble. Have you ever run errands with four boys? It is like herding cats.

My reply went something like, "Boys, this is going to happen, so I need you all to get in the car as quickly as possible. I have no idea how long this will take or how many stops I might have to make. Who knows, maybe we will all go out for a treat. The sooner we go, the sooner we get back home. Let's all get in and just enjoy the ride."

I knew the plan, but the amount of time the plan would take depended on things outside my control: how long would we need to find each item while minimizing fighting, locating stray children (think Costco with samples), and accomplishing everything on my mommy list, which I rarely remembered to make.

Trust that *God knows the plan*; he is moving the pieces into place so you can get in the car and enjoy the ride! *He is keeping the plan safe for you.* If all you had to work with were these two things, it would be more than enough. But there is so much more. There is another piece you need to know if you are an overanalyzer.

He loves you right where you are.

He loves you before you take a step forward.

He loves you if you take a step backward.

He loves you because you believed.

God the Father loves you because you love Jesus.

You are related, and he wants to have a conversation with us rather than to simply answer the daily quizzes we can get into the habit of bringing him in prayer. We ask for what we need in the context of our relationship.

Allow me to explain. Often when we pray, rather than listen, we offer God options. If we are not careful, our prayer time will begin to sound as though we are giving God a multiple-choice quiz:

Heavenly Father, should I . . . ?

A. Stay in my job.
B. Accept this current job offer.
C. Look for another job.
D. None of the above.

Or maybe it's an easier test:

Am I called to do this or that?
Should I marry him or not?
Should I stay or go?
Should I give or not give?

You get the idea. Imagine what this sounds like. Creator of the universe, here are your choices. Which one is correct? Okay, thank you. That's all I needed. And then there are other times when we strain to listen for his answer and are surprised to hear nothing. I believe that in those times God is saying to us, "Daughter, sit with me. Take a deep breath. Rest in me. Listen to what I have to say, not for what you want to hear. I have planned an adventure. Let's dream together. My options are exciting and limitless. Don't limit my answers to these options of yours. There is more. I have solutions you haven't dared to imagine. My plan will cause you to grow while it prepares you for future things!"

Sometimes his input is practical and, once we hear it, obvious.

For example, when our son Addison was a baby, John and I were planning a vacation. John was adamant that I leave Addison behind so that we could have quality time together as a couple, and I was just as adamant that we should bring the baby because I wasn't ready to give up nursing. John took it to prayer. He asked our heavenly Father, "Do we bring the baby or leave him home?" No answer. John asked, "Is there something else I'm not thinking of?" Immediately another idea came to him. We could bring Addison and hire a nanny through a local church we knew of where we were going. That way we'd get time together *and* I wouldn't have to leave our baby behind. That was just what we did. During his naps, we rode mopeds around a pink island and swam in the coves. I was happy, John was happy, and a young girl was employed and blessed.

Returning to my earlier story, the passage I read in Jeremiah 29 didn't reveal the plan. I didn't hear a booming, "Quit your job!" nor did I hear "Stay in your job!" I just knew God hadn't missed a thing and he had a plan, and that was enough to break the hold of fear that had frozen me into doing nothing. A peace settled over me as I realized that God was in control and that whether I quit or stayed, my world was not going to fall apart. This realization gave me the confidence I needed to step back and assess the situation without the distortion of fear and make a wise decision.

USE WHAT HE'S ALREADY GIVEN YOU

Not all of life's decisions require God's counsel. There are some decisions in life that you can make by just using common sense. It is the reason God gave us a brain. If you are hungry, you don't have to pray about whether you should eat (unless you're breaking a fast). If you see someone else hungry, you don't have to pray about whether you should feed them. Once the confusion of fear was pushed aside, I realized my job decision only required common sense. The office environment was toxic—especially for a baby Christian like me, my husband didn't like what it did to me, I didn't like what it did to me, the pay wasn't good, it wasn't a specialized skill set, I was easily replaced . . . so I gave fair notice and quit. When our confidence is in God, we can move forward with assurance.

The next few verses in Jeremiah also spoke into my situation:

Then you will call upon me and come and pray to me, and I will hear you. You will seek me and find me, when you seek me with all your heart. (Jer. 29:12–13)

I want you to hear these verses as an invitation to a progressive communion with God. When we call out to God, he always answers, "Come." This means we go into prayer with complete confidence. Why not praise him rather than quiz him?

Enter his gates with thanksgiving,
and his courts with praise!
Give thanks to him; bless his name! (Ps. 100:4)

Goddaughter, you have a standing invitation into his presence. Don't be afraid to enter. I've learned it is hard to ask for the wrong thing when I am in his presence. In his presence, my perspective shifts and I find the clarity that I lack in my sometimes crazy head. I can't count the number of times that I enter his presence imagining I need one thing only to discover that there is so much more for me to learn, to live, and to love. I leave with the realization that the only thing I need is him.

For example, when I go into his presence in conflict with someone I feel has wronged me, I find that my part in the matter is revealed. If I've been wounded by someone's word or deed, he always probes deeper so I can discover why it hurt me and where they might be hurting to have done or said such a thing. Sometimes it is as simple as a misunderstanding. With these obstacles cleared away, healing begins. In his presence, I hear ways to move forward in strength: *love, forgive, humble yourself, pray for them.*

Allow gratitude and praise to open your heart. Sing your way in! Play music, and as you sing, thank him for what he has done. Bless him for who he is. Worship transcends any barrier; when our hearts are open, no door is shut. This dynamic of thanksgiving can happen as we open the Bible and meditate on the wonder of our God and his great love, justice, and sacrifice. Need something to ponder?

> For the LORD is good;
> > his steadfast love endures forever,
> > and his faithfulness to all generations. (Ps. 100:5)

We can trust that he is faithful to the future generations we will never meet on earth. Our Father is good . . . all good. His love does not waver or thin out and diminish as it extends forward and forever to all generations. He doesn't love you the most the day you are born again and later see you as a disappointment. Our Father loves us perfectly and completely in order

When our hearts are open, no door is shut.

to perfect and complete his work in us. He sees who you are becoming; his sight is not limited to who you have been or even to who you are in this moment. God loves us into who we really are.

Let me bring this idea into a more practical setting. When John and I are both home and I want to talk to John but don't know where he is, I call out his name. He answers, I go to him, and we speak to one another. Easy, right? If John doesn't answer me, it is because he is already talking to someone else or he has headphones on. He rarely hears me call his name and then hides or runs off (just a few times during a fight). He listens for my voice and is excited to talk with me. He hears my heart and I hear his. Jesus echoed this promise of the Father in an even more expansive way:

> Ask, and it will be given to you; seek, and you will find; knock, and it will be opened to you. For everyone who asks receives, and the one who seeks finds, and to the one who knocks it will be opened. (Matt. 7:7–8)

Goddaughter, listen to this glorious promise of our Savior; when you ask, it is given, even when you don't see, hear, or feel it. We are heard, and an answer is set in motion. The phrase *will be* describes a future-tense answer rather than an instantaneous one. Even though his response to us is immediate, there is usually a pause before we receive the answer. Stuff needs to happen. Pieces and people need to be moved into place. There is preparation that needs to take place in us. There are times when we ask for what we *want*, and God has something better in mind for us; he gives us what we *need*. *Seek, and you will find* implies a future tense. Looking back over my life, I found God to be faithful, just, and true, but I rarely saw it in the moment. He answers in his way and timing, not ours.

When we look back, we see what we missed when we were mired down in the moment and looking for a way out.

Goddaughter, just as he has been to me, he will be to you. Trust him when you don't know what to do.

When you pray, he hears. When you seek, you find. When you search with all your heart, your heart finds its home. Making lists and giving God a quiz is searching with your head rather than with your heart. There are times when I pray and hear nothing, yet I have peace because I know my Father is good and I was heard and he has a plan—it's for growth and good.

> When you pray, he hears. When you seek, you find. When you search with all your heart, your heart finds its home.

Start where you are with what you have. Trust that God is not trying to mislead or trick you. Surrender your troubled heart to him and confidently declare, "Father, I am moving forward in faith. If I am not headed in the right direction or if my timing is off, then feel free to stop me and turn me in the right direction."

Then ask for what you need.

What happens if we ask amiss? Guess what? God has a provision for that as well. The book of James tells us,

> You ask and do not receive, because you ask wrongly, to spend it on your passions. (James 4:3)

We recently had the entire family with us for Christmas. Pretty much every hour, one of my children or grandchildren asked for candy. If I knew it was too close to the next meal, I didn't hesitate to tell them no. How much more will our Father deny us what will ultimately feed the wrong things into our lives? Especially if they are ultimately destructive. In the same

59

way, if we do not ask according to his will, God loves us too much to answer those types of prayers.

> And this is the confidence that we have toward him, that if we ask anything according to his will he hears us. (1 John 5:14)

What if we don't know what his will is? We have two guides.

> The Spirit and the Word must be combined. If I look to the Spirit alone without the Word, I lay myself open to great delusions also. If the Holy Ghost guides us at all, He will do it according to the Scriptures and never contrary to them.
>
> George Mueller[2]

Scripture should anchor and confirm what the Spirit whispers. We find his will in the sacred Scriptures. We have written testament if we want to know what his will is: his Word is his will. So, to begin with what we know, we must know his Word.

> If you abide in me, and my words abide in you, ask whatever you wish, and it will be done for you. By this my Father is glorified, that you bear much fruit and so prove to be my disciples. As the Father has loved me, so have I loved you. Abide in my love. (John 15:7–9)

What does it mean to abide in? According to Merriam-Webster, *abide* means "to bear patiently, to endure without yielding, to wait, to accept without objection, to remain stable and in a fixed state of persistence."[3] The opposite of *abide* is to leave, quit, and walk out.

True godmothers will always point you to the Word of God and to the heart of the Father. For me, there wasn't some big moment when I realized exactly what I was called to do. I just did what was in front of me while following what Jesus said.

I love what someone shared with me on social media. She said, after seeking God in earnest for what his call was on her life, she found herself frustrated and without any clear direction. When she was able to still herself, she heard the Holy Spirit whisper, "I've called you to love people."

Doesn't that sound just like Jesus? Simple yet profound. This ability to love others begins with accepting his love for us. Because he loves you, you can love them.

Of course, it is almost impossible to give what you do not have. Do you know that God loves you? I mean the real you. The selfish, impatient you. The flawed, failing you. The one you don't post on Instagram. The silly you, the mean you, the frightened daughter. He loves all that is you. He is not waiting for you to fix yourself so he can love you. It is his love that is fixing you.

Love never fails.
Love begins with who you know.
Love your spouse.
Love your children.
Love your friends.
Love your neighbor.
Love the people you work with.
Love the stranger.
Love people going through difficult things.
Love when it's difficult.
Love difficult people . . . they are the ones who need it the most.
Love people whose lifestyle and faith you disagree with.
Love your enemies; love is not an endorsement of what they do.
Love is God's command. Because love is the fail-safe answer.

Godmother Conversation Starters

Have you been giving God quizzes?

What is one thing you have been afraid to ask for? Dare to ask for it now.

Who is someone you've been afraid to love?

Four

When Healing Is What You Need

Bless the LORD, O my soul,
and forget not all his benefits,
who forgives all your iniquity,
who heals all your diseases.

—*Psalm 103:2–3*

Even though God tells us to ask for what we need, we often hesitate to ask when it comes to the subject of healing. Perhaps we've experienced disappointment in the past when things didn't happen in our timing or way. But never doubt God heals.

He heals in his way, not ours.

He heals in his time, not ours.

He heals in this realm or the next.

I know there are those who will say otherwise.

Perhaps they forget God is the Benefactor who assists us when we cannot assist ourselves. When it comes to healing, forgetting can be dangerous. It can cause us to question everything when we don't understand who he is. It is crucial that we remind ourselves how wonderful the one we call Lord and Father truly is. One benefit is that he aids us in our time of need. The Message reads,

> O my soul, bless GOD,
>> don't forget a single blessing!
>
> He forgives your sins—every one.
>> He heals your diseases—every one. (Ps. 103:2–3)

Because we humans can be forgetful, there are times when you need to speak to your soul and remind it to bless God. This psalm of David opens with,

> Bless the LORD, O my soul,
>> and all that is within me,
>> bless his holy name! (Ps. 103:1)

David spoke to his soul and addressed all his inner being charging them to bless and fully embrace the wonder of God.

For the moment, let's push aside the issue of healing and answer two other questions. Do we believe God can protect us when life seems out of control? Do we believe our Father forgives *all* our sins or just some of them?

Our best reminder of God's protection and provision is found in Psalm 91. When we feel anxious and unable to see God's protection, we have these words to pray and believe:

> Those who live in the shelter of the Most High
>> will find rest in the shadow of the Almighty.

This I declare about the LORD:
He alone is my refuge, my place of safety;
   he is my God, and I trust him.
For he will rescue you from every trap
   and protect you from deadly disease.
He will cover you with his feathers.
   He will shelter you with his wings.
   His faithful promises are your armor and protection.
Do not be afraid of the terrors of the night,
   nor the arrow that flies in the day.
Do not dread the disease that stalks in darkness,
   nor the disaster that strikes at midday.
Though a thousand fall at your side,
   though ten thousand are dying around you,
   these evils will not touch you.
Just open your eyes,
   and see how the wicked are punished.
If you make the LORD your refuge,
   if you make the Most High your shelter,
no evil will conquer you;
   no plague will come near your home. (vv. 1–10, NLT)

And what about our sins? Are there any sins too dark or tainted for the blood of Jesus to cleanse? Or maybe this question touches a more intimate space. Are your sins beyond the power of his redemption? Or do we imagine sin no longer exists, and therefore we have no need of forgiveness and cleansing? Does God become less because we choose to see him in that light?

No on all accounts! A thousand times no. There is no sin beyond his pardon; there is no breach he cannot span.

We know that God is capable of transforming the most scarlet of sins to radiant white. The most profound healing

Prayer acknowledges who God is and invites his involvement in our lost and broken world.

happens when the old is made new and eternity enters our hearts. Why would the healing of a body be any different?

I've seen broken marriages, friendships, and relationships healed.

I still choose to believe God heals even though I've seen friends grow worse rather than better after prayer.

Yet I pray, because prayer is not issuing directives to God so that he might do our bidding. Prayer acknowledges who God is and invites his involvement in our lost and broken world.

God is not obligated to heal *when* I think he should.

God is not obligated to heal *how* I think he should.

At times, God heals through doctors and medicine.

Other times, God heals through a radical change of lifestyle or diet.

There are times when God heals people through prayer.

I've seen people healed physically after they forgave and canceled what held their body bound in bitterness.

Other times God heals and makes them whole in heaven.

I cannot deny the things I have seen with my eyes and touched with my hands. On these pages, I will share the stories that I know. These are not fairy tales. They are testaments to the power of the living God.

A PERSONAL HEALING

When I heard the gospel for the first time, I was twenty-one years old. I surrendered my very broken life to the lordship of

Jesus Christ, and I was reborn. After we prayed, John declared, "Now you're saved."

I really had no idea what he meant. What was I saved from? I asked him, "What does that even mean?"

John replied, "Salvation means you're whole again, spirit, soul, and body."

He had no idea that sitting across from him was a girl whose body was controlled by a cruel eating disorder and whose stomach was constantly racked with pain from lactose intolerance.

"So now that I am a Christian, I can eat cheese?" I asked.

John looked confused. I explained, "You said I am now whole, spirit, soul, and body. I have lactose intolerance, but I'd really love to have cheese again."

I associated food with pain. Just that last semester, I had been hospitalized while they performed a battery of tests on me. John took my hands and led me in another prayer. He directed me to repeat the words after him: "Jesus, thank you for healing me of lactose intolerance. Amen."

That was it.

There wasn't a choir, a smoke machine, or someone on a microphone. Just a whispered prayer between two people on a hot summer night in Indiana.

Instantly, I felt enveloped in the love of God, and a warmth filled my stomach. It was as though all the knots that had been there since I was fifteen relaxed and were untied. I knew something had dramatically shifted in my body. I was healed.

The next day, I went out to lunch with a friend, and I told her what had happened. I shared how I'd been born again and healed. We'd been friends for nearly a decade, and she was well acquainted with my reaction to dairy. She watched aghast as I ordered all sorts of dairy products. She suggested that I might be overdoing it and tempting God. But my reasoning was that healed was healed, and if I was truly healed, my body would be able to handle it. We joined hands and prayed and thanked God for our food, according to 1 Timothy 4:4–5:

> For every creature of God is good, and nothing to be refused, if it be received with thanksgiving: For it is sanctified by the word of God and prayer. (KJV)

A little more than a year later, God healed me of an eating disorder that had ensnared me since I was fifteen. That one wasn't an instant healing like the lactose intolerance; it was more of a healing journey. God told me to stop weighing myself and put away my scale. He whispered, "You are not what you weigh."

I wrote more of this story in my book *You Are Not What You Weigh*, but I wanted to share some with you here as well. It all began when I came home from school one day and my father called me over to his black leather chair. I could sense that he was appraising me and didn't like what he saw. Between draws on his cigarette, he instructed me to turn around so he could see my backside.

"Lisa, your butt is huge! How much do you weigh?" my father asked.

I shrugged my shoulders and answered, "At camp last summer, I weighed 121 pounds."

"Well, you're not at camp anymore. Go weigh yourself."

He was right. I was nearly 140 pounds. I dutifully reported my weight to my father.

"That's way too much!" he countered, then went on to explain that guys weren't going to ask me out when I looked like this. He mentioned how much better I'd looked the year before and explained that I needed to lose the weight immediately. This all hit home. My short, chubby boyfriend from another school had just broken up with me.

Wrapped in shame and yet another layer of self-consciousness, I went down the dark hallway to my bedroom. Why hadn't I noticed this? I carefully locked my bedroom door, pulled the shades, stripped down to my underclothing, and climbed up on my bed so I could see my body in the mirror over my dresser. I stared at my headless reflection in the mirror, and for the first time I realized I *hated* my body.

That night at dinner, I did not ask for seconds. My father watched every bite I took and nodded his approval when I pushed my plate away before finishing. After my homework was done, I put on my old swim-team sweats and running shoes. It was below freezing outside, but I ran in the dark. My feet crunched their way over the snow-covered ground, my father's words chasing me: *You're fat! No guys are going to like you!*

I shook my head to try to loosen the images of myself. But I couldn't shake them. I was utterly repulsive.

The snow sparkled like ground diamonds, and the frigid air felt like needles piercing my lungs, but I ran until my sides ached and I could go no farther. The next day, I barely ate breakfast. At school, I cut my normal lunch consumption by half and again reduced what I ate at dinner. I began to read the articles in my mother's fashion magazines. As I scanned the images of women I could never be as tall or as thin as, they seemed to mock me.

The weight began to drop off. Suddenly, I was noticed. I was complimented. I was flirted with. My father was proud again, and somewhere in my mind, I made a faulty connection.

When I am thin, I am worthy of attention.

When I am thin, I am in control.

When I am thin, I am successful.

Yes, it is right to eat healthy and exercise.

But I was not nurturing my body; I was punishing it.

I did not love my body . . . I hated it.

I learned the hard way that the voice of an eating disorder masks itself as a caring friend or personal trainer, but the narrative quickly turns to the accusations of a hateful tyrant.

Once I became a Christian, I stopped the pattern of excessive deprivation and rebounded with bingeing, and the numbers on the scale began to climb again.

God wanted to work a healing in my life and the catalyst was a personal catastrophe. I was a few weeks away from my wedding, and I had gained so much weight that I no longer fit into my size 10 dress. I was overwhelmed by frustration with myself and anger with God (I'd become a Christian, and now I was fat—as though I was doing God some favor or he was the one forcing me to eat entire pizzas!). Even I realized that line of reasoning was ridiculous.

I was the problem.

And then there was the fear of my father.

How would I tell him? My heart began to race.

God interrupted my panic and asked me to surrender my weight and all my craziness to him. I had a keen sense that he was waiting for me to invite him into this area of my life. Wasn't my weight just a carnal, fleshly area? Why would the God who created the universe bother speaking into my eating disorder?

Anything that holds his daughters captive is important to our Father. He assured me, "I am the one who made you. I'm the one who knows what you should weigh. None of these diets can heal you, and no scale can accurately measure you. Stop weighing yourself. Stop dieting and give this area of your life to me. Your weight is an idol in your life." Images of a golden calf described in my Bible flashed through my mind.

"When you are lonely, you eat. When you are angry, you eat. When you are bored, you eat. When you are depressed, you eat. When you are happy, you eat." He continued, "You do not come to me. You do not read my Word. You eat because it is easier. Repent of giving your strength to and drawing your strength from this idol. I am your strength."

Anything that holds his daughters captive is important to our Father.

I saw it. I saw it all. The years of wasted time and energy became evident to me. Through tears, I mumbled a prayer of repentance and confession. I renounced every vain thing that the Holy Spirit brought to remembrance: *I surrender all of it to you. I can't do it. Father, show me what I should weigh.*

A number flitted across my mind. It was a weight I'd never actually been as an adult. I scribbled it onto a scrap of paper, and I tucked it into my Bible. Then I heard God's Spirit direct me, "It's time for you to fast."

I was confused. Wasn't a fast just a starvation diet? I'd already tried those and failed.

He continued, "Lisa, a diet changes the way you look, but a fast changes the way you see. If you want to be free, you need to change the way you look at everything."

This wasn't about weight loss; it was about tearing down the idols in my life and focusing on my heavenly Father.

I put the scales in the attic, tossed the laxatives and diuretics, and went to the store and bought what I would need for a three-day juice fast. During this time of fasting, I listened

carefully to my body, which was easy because it was screaming! To escape its insistent cries, I filled my mind with worship
music and picked up some spirit swords by echoing the words
of the apostle Paul:

> But I discipline my body and keep it under control, lest after
> preaching to others I myself should be disqualified. (1 Cor. 9:27)

For too long I had allowed the cravings of my body to master my life. After three days, I began to eat again, praying that
the Holy Spirit would show me when I was satisfied. I had to
break the pattern of eating until I was engorged or in pain. It
was a daily discipline. I went for long walks, noticed nature,
breathed prayers, and listened to worship music. The weeks
passed, and I sensed my body growing stronger with each day.
But still, I didn't weigh myself. My wedding week was upon
me, and I sensed fear trying to rise within me. *What if I start
eating and I can't stop again?*

I just stayed the course, prayed over my food, and remained
in tune with my body to know when I was satisfied. On my
wedding day, I wore the dress. It actually hung loosely. As I was
leaving for my honeymoon, the Holy Spirit nudged me to weigh
myself. I climbed up into the attic access from my bedroom and
got down the scale. Closing my eyes, I stepped on the scale.
When I opened them, the needle landed on the exact number
I'd hidden in my Bible. I was healed.

I don't own a scale anymore—not because it is wrong to, it's
just that I don't need to. God has been faithful to keep me strong
and free rather than skinny and weak. Healing came when I repented of my idolatry and turned to my heavenly Father for life.

Both healings were nearly forty years ago, and I am happy
to say that I eat as much cheese as any good Italian should!

THE HEALING OF A SON

When it came to our children, we always involved prayer, but that didn't mean we didn't take them to the doctor or give them proper nutrition.

Alec is the third of my four sons. I'm guessing that is one of the reasons I didn't pay more attention at the time. If he'd been the firstborn, chances are I might have caught on earlier. But I didn't. The other reason for my epic mom fail might have been that he was always looking for ways out of the task at hand. He only brought up the "bump in his mouth" when it was bedtime or when there were chores or homework to be done. And often, it was a heady combination of all three.

Alec was in third grade when I took him for his yearly dental checkup. I was mindlessly leafing through a magazine in the waiting room when the dentist called me back into the examining room. The room felt serious, and I assumed Alec had a cavity. Not so.

"Mrs. Bevere, your son has a large tumor growing under his tongue."

Shock registered on my face.

"Mom, I tried to tell you," Alec reminded me.

"Show her," the doctor prompted.

My son lifted his tongue, and in the bright glare of the dental lights, I saw something that resembled a mushroom. The growth was about the size of a small child's thumb, and emerged at the base of the underside of his tongue. I was horrified. How could I have let this happen? The doctor must have recognized the mommy terror. He assured me, "It's not cancerous, but these tumors have a very aggressive growth pattern. Left unchecked it could compromise his ability to speak. It needs to be removed." The doctor's voice was

grave. He was making sure that I wasn't missing the point this
time.

Heck yes! I wanted that thing out of my son's mouth immediately! I wondered if they would freeze it like a wart. Imagining
that the doctor was waiting for my permission, I said, "Agreed.
Please go ahead and remove it."

"I can't," the dentist explained.

We were immediately referred to a specialist. The dentist's
office called and made an appointment for us for later that week.
I imagined they were not going to leave it in the hands of such
a reckless mom. On the drive home, Alec was quick to remind
me how many times he had tried to show or tell me about it. I
felt sick to my stomach.

When we got home, Alec repeated the story and showed it
to all his brothers. They touched it and, in the way only guys
can, celebrated its grossness. John was out of town, and I was
very troubled because I felt as though an alien was growing in
my son's mouth.

Later that week, we went to the specialist. As he examined
the underside of Alec's tongue, he expressed a concern that the
tumor's root might be deeper than it looked. He probed Alec's
mouth, feeling for where his tongue ended and the tumor began.

"He may lose some of his tongue," the doctor volunteered.
"We won't know for sure until I get in there."

"Will it affect his speech?" I asked.

"It's hard to tell."

I found this lack of clarity disturbing.

The doctor turned to Alec and began to explain that after
the surgery, all he'd be able to eat would be ice cream and milk-
shakes. Alec lit up. Before leaving the office, we scheduled two
more appointments: the pre-op and the operation.

In the car, Alec was listing off the flavors of ice cream I'd need to get *only for him.*

John came home from his trip, and Alec showed him the tumor. I had filled John in over the phone on what was going on, but this was his first time seeing it.

"Wow, I think we should pray," John volunteered. "I don't want Alec losing part of his tongue."

I agreed, but Alec did not. There was ice cream in the mix.

"I promise to buy you ice cream either way," I said.

That night, after all the boys were in bed, John brought his Bible into Arden and Alec's room. He began to read from the book of James.

> Is anyone among you sick? Let him call for the elders of the church, and let them pray over him, anointing him with oil in the name of the Lord. And the prayer of faith will save the one who is sick, and the Lord will raise him up. And if he has committed sins, he will be forgiven. Therefore, confess your sins to one another and pray for one another, that you may be healed. The prayer of a righteous person has great power as it is working. (James 5:14–16)

He spent time telling Alec the meaning of these verses while his younger brother, Arden, listened in on the bottom bunk. When John felt certain that Alec understood what the book of James was talking about, he said, "Alec, did you know I'm an elder in the church?"

Alec shook his head, indicating he had no idea.

John continued, "I am going to stand out in the hallway. If you want me to pray for you, call for me."

As John exited the room, my mommy heart started to beat faster. Was John really an elder? What if Alec didn't get healed?

Would he be devastated? What if oral surgery was the best course for his healing to happen? And then, of course, there was the ice cream. I followed John out to the hallway and tried to whisper a few of my concerns to him, but he waved me off and motioned for me to be quiet. We waited in silence for what seemed an eternity. Then we heard, "Dad!" Alec was calling.

John entered the room while I trailed silently behind like a doubting Thomas. I listened as Alec confessed his sins to his father. It was so precious and innocent. Then John prayed for Alec and anointed him with oil. John spoke to the tumor and commanded it to dry up and disappear, informing it that it had no place in Alec's mouth. I agreed. Alec opened his mouth. Nothing had changed. We put him to bed and prayed that he would have a healing sleep.

I was all for hoping that the tumor disappeared in the night, but when Alec got up the next morning, it was still there. He was in good spirits when he went to school. I was sad the following day when I let him know that I would be pulling him out early for his pre-op appointment.

The next day when I went to his classroom to sign him out, the teacher questioned why he was going to the doctor. It was obvious that Alec wasn't sick, and since he was a challenged student, they didn't like him missing any more classes than necessary.

"He has a tumor under his tongue. Show Mrs. Lawson, Alec," I encouraged.

He lifted his tongue, but the tumor was completely gone!

"Wait! It's gone! The tumor is gone!" I shouted. It had been there when he left the house that morning.

Alec felt around in his mouth. Sure enough, there was no trace of the tumor. "Do I still get ice cream?" Alec asked.

"Yes, we will get lots of ice cream!" I answered.

God had more healing for Alec though. When Alec was in junior high, rather than deepening, his voice became high pitched and shrill until he sounded like Mickey Mouse. He was always messing around and mimicking voices, so at first we thought he might have torn his vocal cords, but resting his voice didn't seem to help it at all. We visited specialists, tests were done, but there was no solution. We pursued natural protocols, and still nothing worked. We came to the place where there were no other options.

Over time, we got used to his voice. But it pained my heart because that was not the case for others. When Alec spoke, people turned their heads in disbelief. It sounded like a cartoon character was speaking out of a teenage boy's mouth. Kids made fun of him. Once, in an elevator, one of his brothers may have come to his defense in a less-than-appropriate way. This went on for years.

In the midst of all this, we continued to pray. Alec prayed, and we prayed for healing and wisdom. Alec moved on from middle school and was now in high school.

Then in 2007, our family went along with John to Australia to attend the Hillsong conference that John was speaking at. The conference took place over the Fourth of July, and Alec had rushed the stage when they asked if there were any Americans in the audience. As they interviewed him, his high-pitched voice was clearly heard reverberating through the stadium of ten thousand people. They asked him to sing "The Star-Spangled Banner" in the key of C. I heard Alec protest, and my heart froze. But it was really a lip sync. I am so thankful they recorded the moment and captured it on YouTube because everything was about to change.

On the last night of the conference, the entire gathering took communion and prayed for one another. It is probably no surprise that we got as many people as possible to pray with Alec. And again, just like before with the tumor, nothing happened. Alec celebrated his sixteenth birthday while he was there, and they gave him a special cake. The next morning was an extremely early start, as we all needed to pack up and catch an early flight back to the States. I was concerned that the boys might oversleep, so I called their room.

A stranger's voice answered the phone. I apologized and was in the process of hanging up when I heard, "Mom?"

"Yes," I answered hesitantly, partly because I wasn't completely awake and partly because I knew I was a mom, just not *their* mom.

"Don't hang up, Mom; it's Alec."

His voice was deep and resonant like a radio host or sports announcer. I heard his sleepy brothers waking up in the background. One of them chided him. "Alec, stop doing fake voices."

But this voice was no fake.

Overjoyed, he ran down the hall and into our room in his boxers! John and I kept grabbing him and making him talk. His voice was strong, beautiful, masculine, and it was Alec's. If I was ever tempted to doubt that God heals, all I'd have to do is go to the recording of my son speaking three days earlier. As a mother of four males, I know that boys' voices do not completely change overnight. But they do when God heals them. We never learned what it was that had so distorted and diminished his voice. It doesn't matter now because he was healed by the name that is above any medical term, fungus, or nodule that could be named.

As I write this, Alec is a grown man. He acts, preaches, and creates short films. His voice has not faltered, and the tongue tumor never returned.

When I say that God is a healer, I am not in any way saying that we shouldn't go to doctors. I thank God for doctors. But doesn't it seem silly not to consult the one who wove us together in our mother's womb? We believe you should pray and go to doctors. And as far as medical science, all knowledge that benefits humankind comes by the inspiration of the Creator. We have both physicians and the great Physician.

What is harder to mend, a broken heart or a broken bone? The heart is. It is far easier to set a bone than to reset a heart. But what is impossible for humans is possible for God. He alone is the healer of hearts. The very one who can heal our broken spirits and souls can surely touch our broken bodies.

THE HEALING OF DAUGHTERS

Trinity, a dear goddaughter, shared her healing with me, and I love how her story shows God's desire to heal even our most shame-filled diseases. With her permission, I share her testimony with you.

> In fall of 2007, I attended a women's conference in New York City where Lisa was speaking and sharing from *Fight Like a Girl*. I made some dream declarations on my heart that day: to have a healthy marriage and raise five children one day! A couple months later, in the middle of a lonely, isolating season as a single woman, I realized I had contracted herpes from a recent encounter on a date. In that moment of realization, I experienced a deeper and darker pit of shame than I ever have. My immediate thought was of wanting to die. The next thoughts

swirling around in my mind were that I deserved this, it was my bad decision, and these were the fair consequences. My dreams of marriage and family slipped away into the darkness that enveloped me. I immediately hopped in a cold shower to ease the excruciating physical pain, and as I stood there, I heard in my spirit this still, small voice whisper, "I want to heal you."

My hot tears mixed with the ice-cold water, and the grace and mercy I experienced kindled hope. I clung to those words as my lifeline in the following days, and as I was alone in my apartment, I continued meditating on Psalm 103 and reading *Fight Like a Girl*. I happened to be on chapter 15 just then, and I froze as I read of the Holy Spirit nudging Lisa to share his message of healing specifically related to women with sexually transmitted diseases at her upcoming conference. Now, I've been both a bookworm and a follower of Jesus since I was a young girl and had never heard these two topics *ever* mentioned together. Gratitude filled me that not only did Lisa obey and follow that uncomfortable request but also that I was able to read a testimony of a woman who struggled with the monthly symptoms of herpes for twenty-three years and who was healed after that conference.

I believed, I felt seen and heard by God, and the most beautiful words I could've heard with the power to break through my shame were of God's *desire* to heal me. He was full of compassion and he wanted to. I prayed Scripture over myself and believed what the Lord said.

I had moved to Italy as an au pair for six months to take a break from the city, and one ordinary day in the shower as I continued to pray Scripture over myself, I felt a warm tingling cover my entire body, and a supernatural peace washed over me. The fear dissolved, and I knew in that moment I was healed. Years later, I have not experienced symptoms since or needed any treatment or medication in pregnancy or childbirth. I've been married almost four years now to the man I continued to wait for, we have a rambunctious little boy with sparkly, adventurous blue eyes, and we are expecting his baby sister to arrive any moment now. That faithfulness of Father God, friendship of his Son, Jesus, and comforting guidance of the Holy Spirit continues to follow me with signs and wonders no matter what storm I find myself going through.

I was in tears as I read Trinity's story of God's healing. She joins a long line of healed daughters. But maybe you still don't think you can ask God for healing. That you are too far from him.

"I want to heal you."

In the book of Matthew, chapter 15, we find one account of a woman who was desperate to see her daughter healed and delivered. She was an outsider who pushed her way in, and for that reason alone I love this story.

> And behold, a Canaanite woman from that region came out and was crying, "Have mercy on me, O Lord, Son of David; my daughter is severely oppressed by a demon." (v. 22)

She showed up, cried out, asked for mercy, called Jesus Lord, and petitioned him on her daughter's behalf. And what did Jesus do? He completely ignored her.

> But he did not answer her a word. And his disciples came and begged him, saying, "Send her away, for she is crying out after us." (v. 23)

When Jesus didn't respond, she pleaded with the disciples. This Canaanite woman was relentless. The disciples begged

Jesus to send her away. Instead, he explained to the woman why she was to be ignored.

> He answered, "I was sent only to the lost sheep of the house of Israel." (v. 24)

Basically, he told her, I'm not here for your tribe and you're not part of my mission. But this mama wasn't going to take no for an answer, because she had not come for herself, she had come for her daughter.

> But she came and knelt before him, saying, "Lord, help me." (v. 25)

She acknowledged her helpless state while remembering the God who heals. Jesus again denied her request.

> And he answered, "It is not right to take the children's bread and throw it to the dogs." (v. 26)

Ouch.

But in truth, Jesus wasn't being cruel, he was being clear.

He knew he'd been sent to the house of Israel; therefore, she was outside of his focus. The time would come when a door would be thrown wide to the gentiles . . . dogs. That time had not yet come, but somehow this woman, the Roman centurion, and the Samaritan woman all knew how to press through this barrier.

> She said, "Yes, Lord, yet even the dogs eat the crumbs that fall from their masters' table." (v. 27)

Even dogs eat crumbs.

She agreed with him: *I get it, as a Canaanite woman, I'm a dog*. But she didn't allow any potential offense to rob her because she knew a deeper truth. She knew who he was.

When we know who he is, who we are is a small matter. We are not healers; we are those in need of healing. In the same way, when it comes to issues of faith and healing, it matters not who we are, where we come from, or even our religious tribe. We can't earn it with our works. Our focus is the healer, bless the LORD, all my soul, the very one we call Lord. We see it when she calls him "O Lord, Son of David" (v. 22). In his commentary, N. T. Wright explains that "she addresses Jesus as 'son of David,' the Jewish messianic title which the disciples themselves were only gradually coming to associate with him."[1]

> *We are not healers; we are those in need of healing.*

Outsiders become insiders when they call him Lord.

> Then Jesus answered her, "O woman, great is your faith! Be it done for you as you desire." And her daughter was healed instantly. (v. 28)

I can almost see Jesus smile and shake his head in disbelief. *Woman, you know who I am. I am he, and even though you do not presently sit at my table, you have chosen to sit at my feet. It is done. Your daughter is healed.*

Healing is found in the crumbs that fall from his table. Healing takes place in communion with Jesus. When we call Jesus Good Teacher, we invite his instruction. When we call him Good Shepherd, we invite his leading. When we call him Savior, we experience salvation. But when we call Jesus Lord, we experience all that is under the dominion of that name.

Beautiful goddaughter, do not allow disappointment, religion, offense, or unbelief to rob you of all Jesus says he is. What we perceive to be unanswered prayers are really prayers answered in a different way. Let's be godmothers and God's daughters who bravely press in even when we feel that Jesus is silent. Let's fall on our knees before him and cry out for one another, even when his well-meaning disciples are asking him to send us away.

Godmother Conversation Starters

Have you ever experienced healing?

If no, is it hard for you to believe God heals when he doesn't answer in our way or time? If you need healing, what is stopping you from allowing him to heal you now?

Would you have any problem praying for the healing of a friend?

What do the words of Psalm 103 speak to you?

A Prayer for Healing

Dear Heavenly Father,

I come before you now in the name of Jesus. I trust you with every broken, diseased, and wounded area of my life. You are the ultimate healer. I position myself to receive everything you have for me and set my soul at rest that you carry both the timing and manner. For my part I speak to my soul and tell it to echo the words of David in Psalm 103 turned into a prayer: I will bless the LORD, with all of my soul, my mind, my will, and my emotions. I redirect all that is wounded and hurting deep within me to turn to the Holy One, and bless his high and holy name that encompasses all that he is and everything I might ever need! Prince of Peace, Provider, Healer, and Wonderful Counselor. I will pause and intentionally remember all his benefits (make this moment personal) and thank him that there is no sin or iniquity that is beyond his power to forgive. You alone are the one who heals every and all my diseases and uneasiness; you alone redeemed me when my life was a sorry, forsaken pit of destruction. You lifted me out and called me your daughter, then crowned me with your mercy and steadfast love. You satisfied my every desperate longing with your goodness and renewed my youth so that I could rise above the disappointments of life and rise like an eagle in hope, while I soar by faith and in love.

In the name of your holy Son, Jesus.
Amen

Five

Dig Up Your Treasure

Hope is the thing with feathers
That perches in the soul
And sings the tune without the words
And never stops at all.

—Emily Dickinson

Yes, lovely goddaughter, I dare you to cling to this hope. For hope lends wings to your dreams. Hope is an arrow threaded with the invisible cord of faith. Don't hesitate; pull back your bow with all your strength. Shoot hope as far into your future as you can dare to imagine. Though you will not see where the arrow lands, its placement will pull you along.

Sing your way forward, and invite the hope your song awakens to reside in your heart. Let its melody wake you in the morning and wash over you at night. Begin with what you know, and use what you have. For hope and her sister faith love it when you set things in motion.

As a godmother, I'd love to expose some lies that cause us to bury our talents and doubt that God treasures us. Perhaps you've heard some of them:

- Why would you think that your life could ever please God?
- You can't be trusted to dream. You're far too greedy.
- Haven't you messed up before?
- How many times have you been wrong?
- Didn't you think you'd be married by now?

Or perhaps the voice is theological:

- God no longer speaks to his children.
- And even if he did, what makes you think you could hear his voice?
- God doesn't speak through women.
- Why would he want to talk to you?

Rather than risk hope, far too many lean heavily into these lies and allow the enemy to cast shade on their dreams . . . yet dreams of being godly are never from Satan. The enemy turns us away from hope by making it about our inability. Unknowingly, we echo his refrain by agreeing with these lies. We submit to their boundaries and resign ourselves to their limitations. Then we agree with his limits:

That's right, I've failed in the past . . . I'm destined to fail again. What was I thinking? I've been disappointed and disappointing.

Insecure and unsure, you wrap your dream in rags so it will not be recognized. Some go even further; they dig a hole.

Dirt is where we bury dead things.

It is where we hide what we are ashamed of.

It is where we place the things that we are afraid to touch.

Burying is different than planting. We don't water what we bury.

Sadly, most of us don't slip outside by moonlight and dig a hole. We find a more intimate place to hide those dreams and ideas. We slip them into a darkened gap in our heart. At first we experience a strange sense of relief. You assure yourself that under the circumstances and given your track record you have done all you could. The thing you were given will be safely hidden and easy to retrieve when it is required. It is only later that you realize that when you bury your talent, you rob yourself.

When you bury your talent, you rob yourself.

On closer inspection, this concept of buried dreams sounds similar to a parable recorded as our warning long ago. To prepare his disciples for his departure, Jesus told stories that explained the ways of the kingdom.

> For it [the kingdom of heaven] will be like a man going on a journey, who called his servants and entrusted to them his property. To one he gave five talents, to another two, to another one, to each according to his ability. Then he went away. (Matt. 25:14–15)

This was exactly what was about to happen. Jesus is the journeying man who is off to prepare a place for his disciples. With an awareness that he is leaving, he calls his servants and entrusts them with his property. Right away we should see that we are entrusted servants rather than entitled leaders. There is nothing I have that God has not given me. Nothing! This is not a ministry thing; this is a discipleship principle. As his servant, I live under his title, not my own.

According to their abilities, one servant receives five talents, another two, and the last servant one. At the time of this parable, a talent was a measure of weight that was applied to gold or silver. This parable speaks specifically of money, but I believe the principle is more about stewardship and less about money. Therefore, it is a mistake to limit this application solely to the use of money. At the end of the day, capacity and talent are more important than money. Money can be stolen or lost, but what you do with the God-breathed treasure within you is completely in your power to steward. Over time, the concept of a talent has grown to encompass so much more. It can refer to a gift on someone's life, such as their athletic, intellectual, or creative aptitudes. Talent likewise can mean endowment, genius, and faculty. As you ponder this parable, don't limit its application to money; think of it in terms of capacity and gifting as well.

> He who had received the five talents went *at once* and traded with them, and he made five talents more. So also he who had the two talents made two talents more. (Matt. 25:16–17)

The phrase *at once* shows us that both servants had an immediacy of action. They were inspired by the master's confidence in them and acted without hesitation. Pulling from my Italian roots, I'm going to quote the ancient Roman philosopher Cato: "He who hesitates is lost."

When you freeze, the gift of momentum is lost. It is like planting something too late in the season and missing what would optimize its growth. When this happens, time no longer works for you; it works against you. These servants took initiative according to their ability. They believed in his belief in them. In other words, our Father would not give us talents if we were incapable of multiplying them. Remember, he is not trying to trick us; he is trying to grow us. These two took leaps of faith and doubled what their master had entrusted to them.

Our Father would not give us talents if we were incapable of multiplying them.

> But he who had received the one talent went and dug in the ground and hid his master's money. (Matt. 25:18)

Underground talents cannot grow any more than buried coins can. They don't shrink, but as they lay dormant, their potential decreases with each passing day. This may be hard to hear, but it is the truth. It is never right to bury what isn't ours.

> *Now after a long time* the master of those servants came and settled accounts with them. (Matt. 25:19)

If we are correct in seeing ourselves as these entrusted servants, then our "long time" has been more than two thousand years. This means we've had ample opportunity to neglect or nurture our talent. I believe there is an urgent need for all of us to dig up any talent we may have buried in fear and use it in faith for his kingdom. Life has taught me that it is difficult to change our actions until we first change our perspective. The master invited the first servant to give his account.

> And he who had received the five talents came forward, bringing five talents more, saying, "Master, you delivered to me five

talents; here, I have made five talents more." His master said to him, "Well done, good and faithful servant. You have been faithful over a little; I will set you over much. Enter into the joy of your master." (Matt. 25:20–21)

Then the second servant, who received the two talents:

And he also who had the two talents came forward, saying, "Master, you delivered to me two talents; here, I have made two talents more." His master said to him, "Well done, good and faithful servant. You have been faithful over a little; I will set you over much. Enter into the joy of your master." (Matt. 25:22–23)

It is immediately apparent that good and faithful equals growth. In the case of these servants, growth translated to multiplication. As we simply move forward in faith and diligence, God multiplies our efforts with wisdom, opportunity, and alliances. Both of these servants are exemplary stewards. Stewardship is a kingdom principle. Heaven is not a democracy, a republic, an empire, a communist regime, or even a socialist nation. It is a kingdom ruled by our Father, the just and wise King. We all want to hear our King say, "Well done." Nowhere in the Scripture do we hear "well intended," "well planned," or even "well said," only "well done," which indicates that something was completed. Both stewards are living examples of these words of Jesus,

One who is faithful in a very little is also faithful in much, and one who is dishonest in a very little is also dishonest in much. (Luke 16:10)

Do you wonder what your life would look like if you had more? I did. My conversations with God went something like this: "Someday when I have more, I will do more." I didn't realize that I was making excuses and postponing my life, which is just another way of burying talents until the *someday*.

I thought, *Someday when my house is larger, I'll be able to keep it clean.* Wrong. Look no further than how you are currently managing what you have to discover what you'd do with more. This also applies to how we steward our educational opportunities, relationships, employment, and involvement with our community of faith. I remember when I quit work to stay home with my children. Going from a two-income household to one meant we still tithed, but the concept of offerings became foreign. One day, I realized that I had buried what I did have. I dug up two powerful talents that I could use: time to pour into younger women and a closet full of work clothes that I no longer needed that would be multiplied in someone else's life. I immediately began to put them into action.

Are you thankful for the house you are currently in? Do you take care of it, or is it buried in your wish for a bigger house? Even as I type, I see areas where I need to improve my stewardship. I am in a new season when I can multiply what I have through hospitality. With all my boys gone, I am going to gather women. Our Father watches how we navigate our *now*, understanding that it foreshadows our future stewardship of the *eternal more*.

Finally, we come to the sad servant who is our object lesson.

> He also who had received the one talent came forward, saying, "Master, I knew you to be a hard man, reaping where you did not sow, and gathering where you scattered no seed, so I was afraid, and I went and hid your talent in the ground. Here, you have what is yours." (Matt. 25:24–25)

When we don't know our Master's heart, we bury in fear what we should multiply in faith. Not only did this servant make excuses but he also made accusations. This servant blamed his master. He called our good and generous master hard—he accused him of theft! "Reaping where you did not sow and gathering where you have not planted" translates to stealing! How small minded! It is impossible for the One who owns everything to steal. Anything any of us has is on loan to us while our master is away.

> But his master answered him, "You wicked and slothful servant! You knew that I reap where I have not sown and gather where I scattered no seed? Then you ought to have invested my money with the bankers, and at my coming I should have received what was my own with interest." (Matt. 25:26–27)

When we don't know our Master's heart, we bury in fear what we should multiply in faith.

Pause a moment. Do you think our Lord is seriously concerned about a return on his money? Is he low on cash? Of course not! He actually gives all the increase and the entrustment back to the stewards. There is a much larger lesson here. How we handle money reflects whether we can be trusted with weightier things. If this servant had put the money in the bank, then someone else would have paid interest to use it. Then the master said something shocking.

> So take the talent from him and give it to him who has the ten talents. (Matt. 25:28)

Why? He doesn't need it. Why not give the one talent to the servant who had four so he could have at least five? Or throw all the talents together in the mix and divide them equally between the remaining two servants? That would be fair. Yes, but what seems fair to us is not always just. The master explained his decision to give the talent to the one with ten:

> For to everyone *who has* will more be given, and he will have an abundance. But from the one *who has not*, even what he has will be taken away. (Matt. 25:29)

What does this "has" and "has not" refer to? It isn't about money; it's about faithfulness. Faithfulness in God's kingdom never involves hiding, hoarding, or burying. Faithfulness multiplies in order to share. This mandate began in Genesis when God told his sons and daughters to be fruitful and to multiply. He never said be barren and divisive. What is the fate of the one-talent servant?

> And cast the worthless servant into the outer darkness. In that place there will be weeping and gnashing of teeth. (Matt. 25:30)

Yikes! That's a bad day. Goddaughter, here is the good news: this very day, we can choose a different approach.

DIG IT UP

As you've been reading this, have you sensed that you may have buried something in fear that it is time to brush off and put to work? What disappointment was it that caused you to forget that our Father is good? What loss caused you to imagine that he was capable of robbing you? Life is unfair, but God is just.

God measures our faithfulness by what we do with what we have. Think of your talent as a packet of seeds. The first two servants planted their seeds, while the third servant never even opened his packet. Far too many goddaughters are looking at their empty hands and forgetting what was planted in the soil of their hearts. Don't be distracted by what your sisters have and miss out on multiplying what is already in your care.

> If then you have not been faithful in the unrighteous wealth, who will entrust to you the true riches? And if you have not been faithful in that which is another's, who will give you that which is your own? (Luke 16:11–12)

And there you have it. What are the true riches? Let's use our talents for what heaven values most: people. God gifts us to lift others. Romans 12:6–8 tells us,

> Having gifts that differ according to the grace given to us, let us use them: if prophecy, in proportion to our faith; if service, in our serving; the one who teaches, in his teaching; the one who exhorts, in his exhortation; the one who contributes, in generosity; the one who leads, with zeal; the one who does acts of mercy, with cheerfulness.

Gifts are meant to be used! How would you feel if you spent a lot of time finding a gift that was perfect for someone and they never even opened it? Or maybe they opened it and never used it. I understand that there are those who would say that the gifts outlined in Romans have passed away. But, *God gifts us to lift others.* I don't believe it for a second. Do you see anything in this list that seems unnecessary? I sure don't. We *need* all of these gifts to be in operation. Jesus had all of these gifts in operation, plus healing and miracles. He gives these gifts separately so that when we come together corporately, as his collective body, they are evident. People are graced with the gift of prophecy. True prophecy is not fortune-telling, it is foretelling in faith what it looks like for God's kingdom to come and his will to be done. There is a grace to serve, as well as a grace to teach and exhort. There are those who are specifically graced to be generous with finances, and we are all called to be gracious with hospitality. There are leaders who are graced with zeal and vision for the realms of government and business as well as for church planting. And cheerfulness is a special grace for those who do acts of mercy, because sometimes the pain they see can be disheartening. When we operate in our God-given gifts, life is multiplied.

MOVE BEYOND EXCUSES

Not long ago, I posted a short clip on social media in the hope of helping people get unstuck. The majority of people were encouraged, but a few echoed back some of my old fears.

What if my desires are not God's?

What if they are just fleshly, carnal desires?

Even worse, what if Satan authored the desire?

My heart actually hurt when I read their words. Have you wrestled with these thoughts? I know I did. You may have different questions, but I fought doubt around all these. I knew that God was good, but I didn't trust myself. This meant I feared any whisper that sounded too much like me.

When we're afraid of succeeding at the wrong thing, we run the risk of doing nothing. We unknowingly bury our talents for fear that we might misuse them. This burial won't sound like a funeral; it will sound like reason. The thought process may sound like this: *God is just and pure, and I am not. I am a worm. I should just be happy I am not headed to hell.*

I also had a plethora of excuses that I paired with my fears of making a misstep. Some, but not all, are listed below:

I am a woman.

I have children.

I have no formal biblical training.

I have no connections.

I have no influence.

I have one eye.

I have a horrible past.

I come from an unstable family.

As I pressed closer into the love of God and the realization that he is good, I discovered these excuses simply masked the list of deeper fears mentioned above that threatened to drown me in their what-ifs. What if my desires are not God's desires? Well, what if they are? What if they are just my own fleshly, carnal desires? Well, what if they are not? After all, my heart can't be trusted. What if it can be?

> When we're afraid of succeeding at the wrong thing, we run the risk of doing nothing.

Let's open some discussion around this. Yes, before you were born again, your heart could not and should not have been trusted. The prophet Jeremiah described the unregenerate human heart this way:

> The heart is deceitful above all things,
>   and desperately sick;
>   who can understand it? (Jer. 17:9)

Notice this verse is a question, which begs an answer. If we can't understand or heal the heart, is there someone who can? I believe there is. We find our answer in the very next verse:

> I the LORD search the heart
> and test the mind,
> to give every man according to his ways,
> according to the fruit of his deeds. (Jer. 17:10)

In other words, our God who can't be missed, who doesn't miss a thing and has your back, had a plan to remedy our hopeless dilemma of deceptive hearts. These are very *big* problems that required a *radically* big answer.

The first answer was Jesus. He was and is the final and *only* solution. Before the redemptive work of Christ, there was no hope. Our twisted, darkened hearts were beyond our human ability to heal. We couldn't fix the mess that our hearts had become. If we could have, God would have left us to do it, but we couldn't. Without Christ we are hopeless messes. It is impossible to be Christlike without Christ. Before becoming goddaughters, we were daughters of death who had lost their way, and our deceptive hearts of stone couldn't be trusted to guide us home any more than a broken compass. Sin partnered with all manner of man-made religions to shame us even as it corrupted our senses and stole our innocence.

Our impossible condition required an impossible remedy . . . we needed a new heart and spirit. For this exchange to happen, someone utterly innocent would need to die for a people who were no longer worthy to live. Not once but twice in the book of Ezekiel, it is prophesied how the Messiah would remedy our impossible dilemma. We read,

And I will give you a new heart, and a new spirit I will put
within you. And I will remove the heart of stone from your
flesh and give you a heart of flesh. (Ezek. 36:26)

When we are born again, we receive the gift of a new heart
and spirit. But he doesn't just give us any spirit; he gives us his
Holy Spirit. The very next verse reads,

And I will put *my Spirit* within you, and cause you to walk
in my statutes and be careful to obey my rules. (Ezek.
36:27)

This new heart and God's Holy Spirit change everything.
You can trust God's Spirit. The Spirit will cause you to walk in
God's statutes and follow his rule. God gave us a heart trans-
plant at the time of our rebirth.

My new heart no longer wants what my old heart wanted.
And the same is true for you. Transformed life flows from transformed hearts.

Goddaughter, hear me:

Wanting a family is not ungodly.

Wanting to be loved is not worldly.

Wanting to have purpose is a God-given desire.

Wanting to be able to provide for your family and be
a blessing to others is godly.

This doesn't mean that there won't be times of confusion
and areas of disappointment. Case in point: not everyone who
wants to be married marries, and not everyone who is married
is happy. The good news in all of this is that we don't have to

be afraid. Rather than draw back, afraid of God or ourselves, our Father invites us closer:

> Let us draw near with a *true heart in full assurance of faith*, with our *hearts sprinkled clean from an evil conscience* and our bodies washed with pure water. Let us hold fast the confession of our hope without wavering, for he who promised is faithful. (Heb. 10:22–23)

The deceptive empty heart has been made true and filled with faith. God keeps his promise. It may look different than how you imagined it, but it will be in keeping with his Word. The one who has promised is faithful. I have walked this earth for six decades, and I promise you that even though you can't go back, anything lost can be redeemed.

I'm not asking you to trust yourself; trust the One who leads you.

Be faithful. Being faithful doesn't always mean being highly visible. Some of the most faithful people are those we imagine are unseen. In this season, I have a microphone and a stage, but I'm well aware that I'm surrounded by people who have been more faithful with things unseen. I remember being in Moscow for a women's conference, and I couldn't help but notice a much older woman in the crowd. Her hair was white, and her face was radiant. After the service, I asked my interpreter if I could possibly speak with the older woman. That was when I learned that I was walking pathways paved by her prayers for the daughters of her nation. Which is harder—walking the path or creating it? I may have been the one talking, but she was the one with the harvest.

Because God is faithful, he corrects my course when I veer off the path. I have seen him bypass the desires of my head to give me the desires of my heart. Hearts hunger for holiness and transformation while heads will settle for affirmation and achievement. Trust your heart rather than your head. Lovely one, you are no longer a daughter of death; you are God's daughter of life and light. We are all invited to adopt the mindset of Paul:

> I don't depend on my own strength to accomplish this; however I do have one compelling focus: I forget all of the past as I fasten my heart to the future instead. I run straight for the divine invitation of reaching the heavenly goal and gaining the victory-prize through the anointing of Jesus. (Phil. 3:13–14 TPT)

Our pasts provide us with plenty of reasons to doubt ourselves, but your past does not have the power to negate God's hand on your future. Each day comes with new choices. Making mistakes in the past doesn't mean you will continue to make them in your future. Learn from them, but never allow the failures of yesterday to paralyze you today. If you buried your talent, it's time to unearth it. God will seed you with desires.

Your past does not have the power to negate God's hand on your future.

Your gift might be something nobody in your family has done. But you don't have to work with what only you can provide; work with what only God can provide.

Your time is a gift, and you have a gift. And "as each has received a gift, use it to serve one another, as good stewards of God's varied grace" (1 Pet. 4:10). In other words, *we are gifted to lift.*

Each and every one of us has a gift. It's not just leaders. As a mother, you are gifted to train your children. As a wife, you're gifted to love and serve your husband. In your friendships, you are gifted to serve your friends. In your community, you are gifted to serve your community.

These gifts are his holy empowerment that resides within you, because you are in him.

Goddaughter, God knows the plans he has for you. They are plans to do you good and not to harm you. Trust that he has not set you up to fail. You can unbury that talent and move forward in this knowledge.

The goal of this chapter isn't to identify your gift. That is a task solely within your grasp. For only you have the right to choose to do that. I will say this, you can take tests online and determine some of it, but gifts are rarely discovered in a vacuum. Gifts are not revealed by study; they must be unwrapped. These gifts are birthed in the doing. Gifts are revealed as we work and serve.

Godmother Conversation Starters

Is there a talent buried under a mound of excuses?

What needs to happen for you to unearth it?

Have you been afraid to trust the counsel of your new heart?

Six

Write Your Way Forward

Why, sometimes I've believed as many as six impossible things before breakfast.

—Lewis Carroll

Looking back, I realize that my entire life is a collection of impossible things, and one day you will realize yours is as well. Watching God do the impossible with our possible and turn our mundane into his marvelous is what makes this faith life exciting. By developing the habit of writing your way forward, you'll be able to recognize God's handiwork along the way. Words become signposts as we go forward and reminders of his faithfulness when we pause to look back. I believe writing is an essential key to moving forward. If you feel a moment of panic imagining I am suggesting that you write a book, take a deep breath. I'm not. I want to explore writing of another type because I've come to recognize that this practice has been nothing short of catalytic.

I told you I quit the first job I had after John and I got married, and I was fired from the first two jobs I had after college. I was in my early twenties and, outside of lifeguarding and waitressing, all my job experiences were bad. I felt like a failure. I hadn't even finished my university degree. I began to wonder if I was doomed to fail at everything I tried or never to complete anything I started. John, on the other hand, was an engineer, and I was his temporarily unemployed new wife. I had no idea what I wanted to do, much less what I was qualified to do. I decided to take advantage of the one thing I did have a lot of . . . *time*.

> The discipline of writing something down is the first step to making it happen.
>
> Lee Iacocca[1]

I was in the nothing zone, and I definitely needed something to happen. It was depressing sitting home alone all day in our apartment in a city where I only knew a handful of people . . . who all happened to be at work. One morning after John left for work, I grabbed a legal pad and some colored pens and went outside on our porch to enjoy the Texas sunshine. I decided to discover what I might be able to do by listing what I enjoyed or dreamed of doing.

I had a strong start with activities: scuba diving, travel, surfing, sky diving. All the ideas in the play or adventure classification came fast and easy. Probably because I wasn't afraid of failing in this category. It was the next layer that was a lot more troublesome. I felt stuck, so I prayed and asked the Holy Spirit to guide me, lifting my thoughts in accordance with his will for my life as I echoed David's prayer from Psalm 19:14:

> Let the words of my mouth and the meditation of
>   my heart
>   be acceptable in your sight,
>   O Lᴏʀᴅ, my rock and my redeemer.

I only wanted to pen what he whispered. I quieted my soul and listened for the words that came to my heart. Here were a few of my impossible things: makeup artist, a job involving travel, mother, television producer, student of the Bible, minister on some level, and writer . . .

Each one came with its own argument.

Makeup artist? Why would anyone want you to do their makeup when you can barely do your own? Have you forgotten you only have one eye? Don't you realize how awkward and ugly you are? My pen froze as my mind raced through the images of every bad photo I'd ever taken. Even my wedding photos were a disaster. I closed my eyes and remembered that a makeup artist focuses on the beauty of others rather than on her own. I wrote it down.

A job involving travel? Where would you go? And why would anyone pay for you to travel? I didn't have an answer for either of these questions. All I knew was that I wanted a job that included travel. I wrote it down.

Mother? What makes you think you could be a mother? You barely have a relationship with your own. If you have a daughter . . . you won't know what to do. True. But I am not above asking for help. When I had children, I would simply watch and learn from other mothers. Then, when I knew how to do better, I'd be able to do better. And perhaps I wouldn't have a daughter; maybe I'd have all sons. I wrote it down.

Television producer? You don't have any experience in television. You're completely unqualified. Well, I will learn. I wrote it down.

Student of the Bible? You were never a good student. Your thought patterns are too random. Maybe there are other people like me who need a new perspective. I wrote it down.

Minister? With your past? You're only allowed to speak to women and you don't even like them! But this was not about me. I wrote it down.

Writer? You hate writing papers. Yes, but I love reading. I wrote it down.

Throughout the process of writing the list, I heard other arguments as well:

"No one in your family has ever done any of these things."

"What will they think of you?"

"Who do you think you are?"

"People are going to laugh at this list."

"You don't have the connections to do any of this."

"You don't have the money, education, or experience."

"You fail at everything you try."

"You're too young."

"You're stupid."

"You're lazy."

"You're ugly."

"You're flawed."

I had no idea how ingrained these limits were until I confronted them. Phrases of doubt and accusation sought to undermine every word I wrote and every dream I dared to capture. Lovely goddaughter, I've discovered that the importance of an idea, dream, or hope can be measured by the opposition you experience when you dare to embrace it. Why else was there so much resistance to penning a simple list?

In many ways, my list was an act of defiance. Ground was being taken back from the enemy of my soul as my heart opened a bit more with each word that appeared on paper. Hope gave substance to my faith, and long-forgotten dreams were reclaimed. There are amazing people in my family, but I couldn't allow their stories to dictate or limit mine. John and I were writing a new chapter. In that moment, I sensed a shift even though nothing had changed.

The importance of an idea, dream, or hope can be measured by the opposition you experience when you dare to embrace it.

As I continued writing, the ideas became more specific. It wasn't long before I had a list of nearly thirty items. When John came home, I was excited yet surprisingly shy about sharing my list with him. He was encouraging even though some of the items surprised him. He made suggestions, and there were additions; we laughed, dreamed, and prayed over the list; and for the first time in a very long time, I felt hopeful.

I feel it is important that I warn you: Shelter your dreams when they are in seed form. Be wise and careful about who you share them with. Some dreams are best pondered in your heart. Once your dream is alive with strength, then you can share it more openly.

Almost immediately, things began to happen. The list became the filter that helped me minimize distractions. I now possessed something I had never had before . . . focus.

The first thing that happened was a phone call. An organization was about to launch a television network, and they needed a makeup artist. They asked if it would ever be something I was interested in. Before I could even answer, they informed me that they would pay for my training and hire me on a freelance basis.

I quickly said yes!

I still didn't have a full-time job and was doing bits and pieces of work at a Dallas mall: one bit was tearoom modeling for Saks Fifth Avenue; the other was filling in at a shop. Once, when John was walking with me through a specific department store, he remarked, "I think you should apply for a position in the makeup department."

I was horrified. I was afraid of the women behind these cosmetic counters. I couldn't count the number of times I'd come in for one item and left with far more than I needed or wanted.

"These women would eat me alive," I whispered. "And besides, I don't have any retail experience; they'd never hire me."

But the seed had been planted, and every time I walked through the store, I heard John's voice suggesting I apply. So one day I did. I was surprised when they called me in for the interview.

The department manager asked, "Why should we hire you? You don't have any retail experience."

I wanted to say, "Exactly!" But instead I answered, "As someone who is training to be a makeup artist, I'd actually help the women. Your salesgirls don't. I've come in looking for an eye shadow and left with an eye cream that I didn't even want, then later returned it and avoided the sales associate."

Wait! Did I just insult her team? I could tell she was taken aback.

"I have wanted to build a more approachable team," she volunteered. Then she ran some retail scenarios by me, and we were done. I thanked her for the opportunity to interview and headed home. Now that nagging voice in my head would stop.

She called me the following week and let me know the job was mine if I wanted it. I was stunned. I hadn't wanted it, but here it was being offered to me. If I wanted to move forward in the field of makeup artist, working in cosmetics would certainly help. I accepted the position and started immediately.

The girls were what I'd feared, and more.

I put my head down and worked with all the clients that they deemed below their notice. It wasn't long before the sales representative for the cosmetic line I worked for came in and took me out to lunch. In less than six months, I interviewed for an account coordinator position and was placed over sixteen stores. A year later, I became a promotional representative and was granted an eight-state territory. Two years later, I landed a full-time job as a makeup artist/production assistant for a television network—just about the time I found out I was pregnant with our first son.

> *Words, whether written or spoken, have the power to highlight our paths.*

I don't mean to make it sound like all I did was snap my fingers and it all happened. There was a lot of hard work, travel, and late nights with each of these positions. What I am telling you is that words create pathways. The psalmist declared, "Your word is a lamp to my feet and a light to my path" (Ps. 119:105).

God's Word lights the way for our feet so we can see our path. His Word is not the path—it is the lamp that lights the way. Words, whether written or spoken, have the power to highlight our paths, though I do believe that the written word carries a greater authority than the spoken. One of the many reasons I feel this way is that written words are more permanent. Contracts are not finalized when they are spoken; they become final when documents are drawn up and signed.

Another reason written words are important is that they are easier to find and harder to forget than words we simply speak. If I had only spoken my list, I seriously doubt I would have remembered all of it that night when John came home. I enjoy listening to audiobooks when I am driving, but I love highlighting and earmarking pages and quotes that I don't want to forget in actual print books.

Words have the power to frame our world. All that we know as life began with words. It is impossible to find something that doesn't have a word or name attached to it.

You, lovely goddaughter, are part of a large and beautiful family, and your story is part of our own. I want you to write with a sense of wonder rather than fear. God is too good, kind, and merciful to be portrayed as harsh. This life is but a vapor. A wispy veil that obscures our real life, which begins in the realm of eternity. Each of our life stories follows patterns known as arcs.

THE ARC OF YOUR STORY

Before we explore your story arc, let's define the idea of an arc. Merriam-Webster defines an arc as "the apparent path described above and below the horizon by a celestial body (such as the sun)."[2] In light of this definition, each day is an arc. The darkened sky glows rosy to announce the sun's ascent, then the brightness increases each minute until the sun's zenith fills the sky. Once the day is spent, the sun descends westward, where it disappears in a coral blaze, leaving behind a charcoal sky. The psalmist King David describes this sky dance in Psalm 19:

> What a heavenly home God has set for the sun,
> shining in the superdome of the sky!

> See how he leaves his celestial chamber each morning,
> radiant as a bridegroom ready for his wedding,
> like a day-breaking champion eager to run his course.
> He rises on one horizon, completing his circuit on the
>   other,
> warming lives and lands with his heat. (vv. 5–6 TPT)

I love David's description. It is an invitation to wonder. As we lift our eyes to the sky, we glimpse the goodness of the Creator. David began Psalm 19 with,

> God's splendor is a tale that is told;
> his testament is written in the stars.
> Space itself speaks his story every day
> through the marvels of the heavens.
> His truth is on tour in the starry vault of the sky,
> showing his skill in creation's craftsmanship.
> Each day gushes out its message to the next,
> night with night whispering its knowledge to all.
>   (vv. 1–2 TPT)

You, lovely goddaughter, are part of this dance of splendor. You were created to lift your eyes to the heavens rather than lower them to a screen like a yoked or burdened beast. Before you write a word, invite God's wonder to wash over you. He speaks the loudest in the silent and incomprehensible.

> Their words aren't heard,
>   their voices aren't recorded,
> But their silence fills the earth:
>   unspoken truth is spoken everywhere.
>
> God makes a huge dome
>   for the sun—a superdome! (Ps. 19:3–4 MSG)

Without a word, without a sound, the truth is framed in the marvelous. I challenge you to embrace the expanse. When night falls, set aside your phone and step out into the falling darkness. Take a deep breath and let your heart soar to the stars.

There was a time when we knew we should look to the stars to connect with our Creator. The wise men of the East discovered the birth of the Messiah written in the stars. Our heavenly Father used stars to inspire our father of faith, Abraham.

> Then the Lord took Abram outside and said to him, "Look up into the sky and count the stars if you can. That's how many descendants you will have!" (Gen. 15:5 NLT)

At times God calls us outside in order to enlarge something that needs expansion inside of us. The celestial arcs carry the imagery of stories, orbits, and lives coming full circle.

As the earth spins one thousand miles per hour, we wake, work, love, fight, laugh, cry, eat, sleep, and then wake so we can do it all again. As the sun begins its arc across the sky, we are reminded that every day begins another story, which is powerful and leads me to another definition of arc: "a sustained luminous discharge of electricity across a gap in a circuit or between electrodes."[3]

You've seen this type of arc before. Yesterday I saw a rather frightening display of these arcs in the form of lightning. As a young girl, I created arcs of my own by shuffling sock-covered feet down a dark carpeted hallway, building up electrical ions as I went. When I touched my bedroom doorknob, a spark would appear and the discharge would shock me. It felt like magic. And yet, an arc is more than a spark; it is a sustained bridge of electricity that connects two formerly separate objects with an enormous amount of power. There is power when gaps are bridged just as there is a loss of power when they are breached.

And now we come to the definition of a story arc. Here, the term is used to describe the flow or emotional pattern of a story. The *Atlantic* had a fascinating article, "The Six Main Arcs in Storytelling, as identified by an A.I. [Artificial Intelligence]." Researchers from the University of Vermont and the University of Adelaide fed nearly two thousand stories into computers, and the resulting emotional arcs of stories fell into six main categories:

1. Rags to Riches (rise)
2. Riches to Rags (fall)
3. Man in a Hole (fall, then rise)
4. Icarus (rise, then fall)
5. Cinderella (rise, then fall, then rise)
6. Oedipus (fall, then rise, then fall)[4]

Which of these patterns represents where your life is right now? Whichever it might be, the good news is that in Christ, we end with a rise even if it is not apparent on this earth. Always.

We are created to live out the very things that God has written in our hearts. What was written there? Love, truth, redemption, hope, faith, legacy, and life. Our lives are a collection of so many little stories that join together to form one massive story arc expressed by our individual and collective lives.

ONE THOUSAND WORDS

The average life expectancy of a female is eighty years. Just to make the math easy, many books are eighty thousand words in length. For illustrative purposes, let's pretend that the number of years (eighty) and the number of words (eighty thousand) represent the story of your life; each year of your life could be likened to the writing of a thousand words, which means each day might come out to an average of three words a day. Some days might require more words to describe them and other days might be completely blank. Many times I have had to delete words I'd written the previous day and replace them with better descriptors later. For example, harsh and unkind words might be crossed off and words like "I am sorry," "forgive me," "I love you" would take their place.

Today I choose the word *reflective* and I'm planning on carrying over extra words into my tomorrow.

Yesterday, my words were *tired*, *sad*, and *grateful*.

Tired because I was recovering from an overseas trip.

Sad because in the span of a few hours I heard of two suicides and one tragic accidental death.

Grateful because I was able to give away some of the furniture that our family had used and loved to a young couple who had recently moved here from the Ukraine. As I watched them load the items into their van and drive away, I was grateful that I am in a season when I can give rather than only receive. You may be tired of hearing about the importance of gratitude, but words of thankfulness have the power to fill an empty heart.

As the sun sets on your day, what word would you like to see hover over tomorrow's dawn? Rather than write what has been, let's write what could be. Let's write words of hope. It is never too late to write a new ending to our story.

Our day may look and feel very different than we thought it would when the sun rose in the east. Some days can be captured with a word. If a day has been particularly difficult or wearisome, it is best to whisper the word *done* as you climb into bed, beyond thankful that the arc of that day is over. When my children were little and my husband was gone more than he was home, my word for most days was *blur*. Each exhausting day morphed and bled into the next one. I remember noise, tears, laughter, laundry, kisses, messes, homework, meals, fights, and cuddles. Looking back, I refer to that crazy, chaotic time as the *blessed blur*. Now I see the beautiful curves that I missed in the tension of exhaustion and highly charged moments.

I look out the window and notice that the Colorado sky is painted pastel-edged gray by the setting sun. When I close my laptop tonight, I'll rest and, God willing, step into a new day traveling the same trajectory and adding more words to the story.

What might we write?

Let's begin by framing our days with these words of David:

> Then I said, "Behold, I have come;
>   in the scroll of the book it is written of me:
> I delight to do your will, O my God;
>   your law is within my heart." (Ps. 40:7–8)

Earlier today, I met a woman who'd read the story I had written about forgiving my father. She applied the principle of what I'd said to him in a very difficult season with her husband. I love that my redemptive story became part of healing her marriage. In the same way, I believe there are things in your story that are part of the larger story God is writing.

Rather than focus on what's lost, let's write what waits to be found.

Rather than focus on what's lost, let's write what waits to be found.

Rather than record hurts, let's write what heals.

Before writing what we long for, let's write what we're thankful for.

Let's close some gaps and write our way forward.

Godmother Conversation Starters

Write at least one thing you can do, dream, or give to move you forward.

Write one thing you are thankful for.

Set a time each day to lay down your phone and step outside. Watch the sun rise, watch it set, or count the stars. Listen for the words spoken in silence and write them down.

Seven

Focus Is Your Superpower

*I don't care how much power, brilliance or energy you
have, if you don't harness it and focus it on a specific target and hold it there, you're never going to accomplish as
much as your ability warrants.*

—*Zig Ziglar*

Focus multiplies any and every capability that life entrusts us
with. If fairy godmothers were real, they'd tell you that magic
wands only serve to focus energy. Keep this imagery and skip
the wand because all you need is the right focus.

Keep your eyes on Jesus, who both began and finished this
race we're in. Study how he did it. Because he never lost sight
of where he was headed—that exhilarating finish in and with
God—he could put up with anything along the way: Cross,
shame, whatever. And now he's there, in the place of honor,
right alongside God. (Heb. 12:2 MSG)

Focus directs or redirects our energy and gifts toward a goal. Our goal is transformation. In a world screaming, "Be like us!" we focus on him. What we behold we become, and where we look is where we go. It is hard to become more like Jesus if we give more time and attention to people and images on any given form of social media. It is extremely dangerous, and I would go so far as to say a form of idolatry if our goal is to play to an anonymous audience (social media) to the neglect of the audience of one. Becoming like Jesus is both our beginning and our end. Not likes, purchases, downloads, follows, or views. If that goal has been displaced, then it is time to set some other things aside. We finish in and with God. It is comforting to know that the One who made a way is the very One who is with us all the way. This is not always the case with people. Life happens, there is loss, seasons change, relationships shift, popularity rises and falls. There is but one constant. Another version of this verse says that Jesus is the "author and the finisher of our faith" (KJV). Unlike some of us, Jesus always finishes what he begins. Resets empower us to renew. Focus helps us to align our lives with what is truly important.

> Do not be conformed to this world, but be transformed by the renewal of your mind, that by testing you may discern what is the will of God, what is good and acceptable and perfect. (Rom. 12:2)

Mind renewal requires focus. My mind has a tendency to drift. My husband accuses me of getting lost in the weeds and off topic in our discussions. I know who my focus is, but the actual ability to focus is a challenge for me. On any given morning, espresso may be needed to make focus a reality. For me the struggle is so very real, so in this chapter I want to tackle both ways to sharpen our focus and what focusing on Jesus looks like. As a major boy mom who is now the mom of four men, I want to revisit a scene that captures some of the essence of focus for me.

THE MAN OF STEEL

What mama could possibly know more about focusing superpowers than the mother of Superman? In the movie *Man of Steel*, Clark's superpowers are awakened, and he is crippled by an awareness of too much too fast. When this happens, he is in class and can't answer the simple question the teacher has asked him. Even though he knows the answer, he can't get it out because all the interference has paralyzed him. Suddenly, he no longer simply sees people; he sees through them, and the smallest sounds are magnified to unbearable levels. Utterly overwhelmed, Clark runs out of the classroom and hides in the janitor's closet. He is followed by his classmates and his teacher, who bangs on the door, demanding he open it. Clark refuses. He remains hidden in the closet, head bent, ears covered, eyes tightly shut, until his mother shows up. She asks, "How can I help you if you won't let me in?"

With tears in his eyes, Clark answers, "The world is too big, Mom!"

"Then make it small," she whispers. "Just focus on my voice."

It works, and the frightened son, destined to be Superman, leaves the closet and enters his mother's embrace.

The first time I saw this scene, I cried.

If we were face-to-face, I'd pull you close because hugs have a way of making our worlds smaller. In that moment, we feel safe, surrounded, and engaged. Then I'd look you in the eyes and say, "Goddaughter, if your world is too big, let's find some ways to make it smaller."

It is as simple as focusing on God's voice.

We don't need X-ray vision or superheightened hearing to realize that we live in a world overrun by sensory overload. This dynamic can overwhelm the best of us and cause us to forget the very answers we already know. The inability to engage with all that comes your way is not a flaw; it's a fail-safe. We all need the pause and the rest; it is the very reason God created the Sabbath.

I remember that, with the birth of each of my sons, I found myself wanting to pull away from everything and everyone that pulled my attention from them. We needed to bond. The one I had carried within me was now wonderfully and strangely outside of me. Bonding requires one-on-one, focused attention. It's hard to bond in an environment of constant interruptions.

There are seasons when I've sensed Jesus drawing me into a posture of solitude. He pulls me away from the many voices so I become more in tune with his voice.

There is no greater honor than to be invited to sit alone with our Prince.

There is no greater honor than to be invited to sit alone with our Prince.

You, lovely one, have every right to choose how many people, ideas, and demands you let into your life. If you have already let in too much and discover that it has compromised your ability to focus, then you have full permission to pull back and move some things out of the way.

As I searched the web for helpful tips to increase your focus, one of them said to literally use your hands as blinders. You can do this by cupping your hands on either side of your eyes, eliminating peripheral vision and centering your focus. Your visual vantage goes from wide-angle view to telephoto. Your brain reasons that if something can't be seen, then it doesn't require your attention. I tried it, and it works. The sides of my messy desk disappeared, and all I saw was what was immediately before me. It is like cropping a photo to highlight what you want seen.

How do you capture a child's attention? You put your hands on either side of their face and invite them to look at you. Beautiful daughter of the Most High, I want you to imagine your heavenly Father cupping your face in his hands and inviting you to look at him. We are invited to draw near so that everything else might fade away. We have this promise:

> *Move your heart closer and closer to God, and he will come even closer to you.* But make sure you cleanse your life, you sinners, and keep your heart pure and stop doubting. (James 4:8 TPT)

I know this verse is both an invitation and a correction, and that's okay. His presence washes away what life so quickly muddies. It is an invitation to stop messing around with the things that once defiled us and wash our hands of what shamed us. Now that we have a new heart, we want to keep it pure.

> We *look away* from the natural realm and we *fasten our gaze onto Jesus* who birthed faith within us and who leads us forward into faith's perfection. His example is this: Because his heart was focused on the joy of knowing that you would be his, he endured the agony of the cross and conquered its humiliation, and now sits exalted at the right hand of the throne of God! (Heb. 12:2 TPT)

You were his focus and the vision set before him that gave him the strength to go through the suffering of the cross. You were his hope; now he is ours. Jesus first rested so that he could focus. Let's observe his rhythm.

> The next morning, Jesus got up long before daylight, left the house while it was dark, and made his way to a secluded place to give himself to prayer. Later, Simon and his friends searched for him, and when they finally tracked him down, they told him, "Everyone is looking for you—they want you!" (Mark 1:35–37 TPT)

To prepare for a full day, Jesus pulled away. He shrunk his world to secluded time with the Father. Before he gave to the people, he gave himself to prayer. Before listening to many voices, he listened for the One. This is when he gained the insight to know what his Father was doing.

Prayer makes an intimate connection between heaven and earth. Secret places help us recover our focus. This smaller space shelters us from prying eyes and loud voices. It is our closet when classmates are whispering in the hallway. Huge things can happen with small adjustments. For example, don't turn on all the lights in your home when you first get up. Limit what you see and do to a minimum. Pause. Ponder. Do not press the power button on your phone, iPad, or computer. Close out everything that fights for your attention. Then slowly choose what you will allow back in.

My husband, John, goes outside and walks. I sit with a Bible and journal with worship music. It is a place or space in time when we are not thinking of what we need to do next. Our social media is not on our mind. The door is shut to all the demands, and we close our ears to all the demeaning comments, even the ones we tell ourselves.

When you adopt this posture of solitude, the Holy Spirit may bring a Scripture to your remembrance, the words of a song or an idea might come to mind, and you have the tone, direction, and insights you need for the day. This is important because studies have discovered that . . .

> One look at an email can rob you of 15 minutes of focus. One call on your cell phone, one tweet, one instant message can destroy your schedule, forcing you to move meetings or blow off really important things, like love and friendship.
>
> Jacqueline Leo[1]

If that is how disruptive one email can be, how much time and possibly emotional energy does scanning your entire Instagram feed or reading all the incoming texts rob from your ability to not only focus but to create and construct.

FOCUSLESS FOR DAYS

When my children were young, there were busy days filled with activity yet almost completely void of measurable accomplishments. In certain seasons of life, this is normal, but my season morphed into a lifestyle of chaos.

Each night I went to bed exhausted and disappointed, and every morning the failures of my previous day weighed heavily on me. I made lists and promised myself that the next day would be different . . . but it wasn't. The pattern of unfocused frenzy continued unchecked. Each night, John came home to a messy house, a messy wife, and kitchen chaos because dinner wasn't ready. More than once, he asked, "Lisa, what did you do all day?"

Frustrated, I'd fire back, "I don't know, but I have been busy!"

Busy was an honest answer. *Focused* would have been a lie. Every hour of the day found me pulled in another direction. I wasn't watching television or napping. Social media didn't even exist at the time. And yet I was so busy that taking a shower was a major accomplishment, and makeup was a life goal.

The main source of my distraction was the fact that John was a youth pastor (making me an unofficial, unpaid one as well), and our phone number was listed. John worked out of the church, where he did not have a direct line. Our home phone started ringing early in the day, and my life went from one phone call to the next. I thought it was godly and Christian to allow everyone to interrupt my life. I imagined my actions were saintly and selfless, but they turned out to be neither. They were careless. It is wrong to allow those outside your home to control what happens within it. Looking back, I don't believe I was as helpful as I'd imagined. I was never fully present for the people calling me or for my children. I lived in the frantic in-between.

Saying yes to many good things translates to saying no to the most meaningful. Currently, I'm in the last month of writing, and there's been a deluge of last-minute requests for worthy projects. Every one of them is something I would like to do. I waffle because I hate disappointing people, which means I hate saying no. I realized saying yes to any of these would be akin to saying no to finishing my book. This would equate to saying no to my publisher who I am in a contractual relationship with. It would also mean saying no to my husband, family, team, and friends.

To correct this imbalance, I have someone who knows my weaknesses and desires and who acts as a gatekeeper. She edits distractions so I can focus. Maybe you don't have an assistant. That's okay; you can create one.

Make a list and allow your list to act as gatekeeper. Writing things down helps to unburden your brain. A list forces you to focus and delineate between what is primary and what is secondary. As Albert Einstein once said, "Paper is to write things down that we need to remember. Our brains are used to think."[2]

Type it into your phone or laptop; just record it somewhere. Capturing thoughts unclutters your brain, and if you're like me, you'll feel a sense of relief after you have recorded the things that are swirling around in there. This is because your mind is now free to process your ideas. This way your brain energy is directed toward constructing ideas rather than keeping record.

There were times when I embraced distraction because I was afraid to focus or feel something in the moment. Avoidance does not make the issue go away. I find that things I avoid completing or confronting only loom larger until they are addressed. If I am procrastinating, I ask myself, "Why am I avoiding this person, project, or conversation?" "What am I afraid of?"

The answer may be that I don't have what I need to start. Or it might be that I am afraid to start because I don't think I have what it takes to finish. Or maybe I've overcommitted, and it has shut me down. Maybe I need help, and I am afraid to ask for it. Maybe I agreed to something that was unrealistic with my schedule. Or maybe I am afraid of the consequences.

Distraction is a wildly successful ploy of our enemy, so it is widely employed. Distraction is his hocus-pocus; it is his bait and switch. Like a magician or illusionist, he wants you to look the other way so you miss what he is doing behind the scenes. Because as soon as you begin to know what you're about . . . the enemy will do his best to turn you about. Unfocused daughters are never really a threat. But once you know what you are aiming for, you will be taken seriously.

Comparison is another form of distraction that robs us. It is such a huge deal that a few years ago I wrote an entire book about it titled *Without Rival*. Comparison breeds confusion and robs people of their purpose because they are so busy looking at who they are not that they forget who they are. But in this moment, let's explore a more lighthearted example.

Imagine that you have finally escaped on a date night with your husband. After a quiet dinner, you go to the movies, and in the course of the on-screen love story, the actor husband kisses his actress wife. Suddenly, the voice of comparison poses a question:

When was the last time your husband kissed you like that?

The man sitting next to you is oblivious. You begin to stew.

He never kisses you like that anymore.

You went into the movie happy, and you leave disappointed. Why? Because you compared your spouse with a pretend man. Now you have a choice: You can pull away and become critical and have a bad night. Or you can grab that man and kiss him the way you wish he would kiss you and have a good night! If having a good marriage is your focus, comparing your husband to Thor, Iron Man, or Captain America will not get you there.

Comparison will lead you down the path of compromise and competition. Believe me, you don't want to go there. Both destinations are distractions.

Comparison is easier to push aside when we realize we serve a God who is beyond compare. We have but one goal, one Instructor, and one life to glorify him with. As I pursue Jesus, I discover who I am becoming.

Recently, a young woman told me that it was difficult for her to finish books, yet she had been able to binge-watch shows. As we spoke, she realized it wasn't due to a lack of time or attention on her part. It was a lack of wisdom when it came to what she chose to focus on. We are admonished:

> My dear friends, this is now the second time I've written to you, both letters reminders to hold your minds in a state of undistracted attention. (2 Pet. 3:1 MSG)

Do you hear the urgency? Peter is saying, "Listen up, people! Time to focus! Things are going to get confusing." The good news is, we have the power of choice! I am in charge of holding my mind at attention just as much as I am in charge of what I choose for my mind to hold.

Good books require good editors. If you want the story of your life to have purpose and meaning, allow wisdom to act as an editor. Wisdom will help you remove the things that distract and detract from what God wants to do in and through your life.

Comparison is easier to push aside when we realize we serve a God who is beyond compare.

Here are but a few of the truly valuable things in life that require attention: husbands, children, rest, and real community.

Having said all this, distractions and interruptions are not always the same thing. Distractions lead you away from your purpose; interruptions can potentially lead you toward it. Okay, sorry if I just made this confusing. Let me try to differentiate between the two.

The other night I hosted our entire family for dinner. I was busy in the kitchen when my youngest grandson invited me to play with him in the nook under the stairs. I can still see his smile and hear his sweet voice: "Play with me, G-Mama!"

I wanted to call off dinner and just sit with August. What I did was join him in the nook; we sat opposite one another and played LEGOs in this small space. I engaged with him as long as I could. It was brief but memorable. As I closed my eyes that night, it was those moments of looking into his green eyes that refreshed my soul.

TELLING A SISTER NO

There are times when saying yes to Jesus means saying no to some sisters. I believe you know this story of Mary and Martha, found in Luke 10.

> Now as they went on their way, Jesus entered a village. And a woman named Martha welcomed him into her house. And she had a sister called Mary, who sat at the Lord's feet and listened to his teaching. (vv. 38–39)

Martha had the right idea. She welcomed Jesus into her home, but it was Mary who made him her focus. Before we go any further, I promise we are not going to make this about Martha and what she didn't do. We are going to look at this interaction with fresh eyes.

> But Martha was distracted with much serving. And she went up to him and said, "Lord, do you not care that my sister has left me to serve alone? Tell her then to help me." (v. 40)

Her frustration is understandable, and serving is not wrong, but Martha missed a moment when she focused on the wrong thing. What was she distracted by? *Much serving.* Martha was okay with doing her part, but she wasn't okay with doing Mary's part as well. If Mary had helped Martha with the service load, Martha wouldn't have been so stressed. She had counted on Mary's help when she welcomed Jesus into her home.

In his book *Surprised by Scripture*, N. T. Wright offers some interesting insights, "Mary was sitting at Jesus's feet *in the male part of the house* rather than being kept in the back rooms with the other women." He goes on to say that in doing so, "Mary had cut clean across one of the most basic social conventions."[3]

Even today, in many Middle Eastern cultures this type of behavior is uncommon, but during the first century it would have been unthinkable. Women weren't meant to be part of the men's conversations. And when Martha points out her sister's error, Jesus endorses Mary's radical behavior.

I love how the Passion Translation depicts Jesus's response,

> The Lord answered her, "*Martha, my beloved Martha.* Why are you upset and troubled, *pulled away by all these many distractions*? Are they really that important? Mary has discovered the one thing most important by choosing to sit at my feet. *She is undistracted*, and I won't take this privilege from her." (vv. 41–42 TPT)

Serving is a good thing unless it removes us from the presence of the one thing.

Undistracted time with Jesus is a privilege. Mary's portion was better than the food Martha was working on. Serving is a good thing unless it removes us from the presence of the one thing. But wait. Do you want to hear something almost too beautiful for words? The Passion Translation is from the Aramaic, and in Aramaic the name Martha means *lady*. So it's not a stretch to read this verse as,

> The Lord answered her, "*Lady, my beloved Lady.* Why are you upset and troubled, *pulled away by all these many distractions?* Are they really that important?"

Now Jesus is no longer speaking to one specific woman named Martha; his words reach into the hearts of all his beloved ladies.

Ladies, his questions are worthy of our reply.

Why are we upset and troubled?

Why do we allow distractions to pull us away?

Did we forget what is important?

Do we resent our sisters who choose to sit with him rather than serve with us?

We lose perspective when our lives are out of focus. This happens when we forget that who we are to Jesus is much more important than what we can do for him. Ladies, we are his first love. "We love because he first loved us" (1 John 4:19). Sitting at the feet of Jesus is a posture of adoration and learning. Jesus loves the distracted and tenderly reminds us: First comes love, then comes service. When we get this backwards, we become easy prey to distraction. Anxiety follows a lack of focus just as a lack of clarity is an invitation to confusion.

We cannot focus on the wrong things and get the right results. When Jesus is your focus, he will take care of showing you the things you need to see. As you pursue Jesus, you find the people and things that require your attention. He is more than capable of causing our paths to cross. When he is our pursuit, we find what we need in his wake. He is a faithful guide.

In Matthew 23, Jesus repeatedly referred to the scribes and Pharisees as blind guides because they majored on minors and minored on the majors. I read it in three versions, but I am highlighting the Passion Translation because I feel it brings the most clarity to what had caused their blindness.

> Great sorrow awaits you religious scholars and you Pharisees—frauds and pretenders! For you are *obsessed with peripheral issues*, like insisting on paying meticulous tithes on the smallest herbs that grow in your gardens. These matters are fine, *yet* you *ignore the most important* duty of all: *to walk in the love of God*, to *display mercy* to others, and to *live with integrity*. Readjust your values and place first things first. What *blind guides!* Nitpickers! You will *spoon out a gnat* from your drink, yet at the same time you've *gulped down a camel* without realizing it! (Matt. 23:23–24 TPT)

If we are not careful, peripheral issues become distractions from the focus of the gospel. Not long ago there was an uproar over whether it was right for women to preach inside of church buildings, behind pulpits, on Sunday mornings. Opinions on this matter ranged all the way from women being able to hold the position of senior pastor to women remaining silent during Sunday services. But at the end of the day, are any of these issues of salvation? Probably not.

Here is my attempt to chart some of these nonessential and essentials:

NONESSENTIAL ISSUE	ESSENTIAL ISSUE
Whether women should preach	Whether Christ is preached
How we worship	Who we worship
How we look	How we live
Our achievements	How we love

NONESSENTIAL ISSUE	ESSENTIAL ISSUE
Our opinions	The truth
Our identity in culture	Our identity in Christ
What we have	What we give
Unity of doctrine	Unity of faith
What we eat	What we say
What culture says	What Scripture says
What others do	What we do
What we study	What we live
The integrity of others	Our integrity
What others believe	What we believe
How we dress	How we clothe the naked
How we've been wronged	How we forgive

Collectively and individually we need to take a good long look at this list and decide what are the essentials that we need to focus on and what are nonessentials that are merely distractions that serve the enemy's purpose to divide and conquer us. It could be that you disagree with some of what I have listed above. That's okay. Or maybe I've forgotten a few items; if so, feel free to make your own deletions or additions. My hope is that Christ rather than our contentions will become the focus.

BLIND BUT FOCUSED

Now let's talk about someone who lost his sight but never his focus. We find his story in Mark 10.

> And they came to Jericho. And as he was leaving Jericho with his disciples and a great crowd, Bartimaeus, a blind beggar, the son of Timaeus, was sitting by the roadside. (v. 46)

This story features Jesus, his disciples, a large crowd, and a lone blind man sitting by the side of the road. Blind Bartimaeus heard a commotion as the crowd exited the city. Something was different. There was joy and excitement in their voices. He heard Jesus was among them. Hope and faith rose in his heart, and almost before he knew what he was doing, Bartimaeus cried out,

> "Jesus, Son of David, have mercy on me!" And *many* rebuked him, telling him to be silent. *But he cried out all the more*, "Son of David, have mercy on me!" (vv. 47–48)

Then not one voice but many voices in the large crowd tried to silence him. Ignoring their protests, Bartimaeus got louder. His behavior should be an example to us all, because the people trying to silence you are not the ones with your answer. They are okay with you staying on the roadside. Don't waste your time or voice arguing

The people trying to silence you are not the ones with your answer.

with them. Some even prefer for you to remain blind. Goddaughters, when people try to silence you, don't yell at them; it's your cue to cry out louder to Jesus!

> And Jesus stopped and said, *"Call him."* And they called the blind man, saying to him, "Take heart. Get up; he is calling you." (v. 49)

Jesus stopped, and the one who'd cried out in the face of opposition was called forth. Pause and imagine what that moment felt like. Everything was about to change and Bartimaeus knew it. Years of darkness were about to yield to visions of light. He was ready.

> And throwing off his cloak, he sprang up and came to Jesus. (v. 50)

Why did he throw off his cloak? Some commentaries say that this particular type or color of garment gave him legitimate begging rights. Bartimaeus knew he would no longer need this cloak because he was no longer a beggar. He was certain Jesus was able to heal him. I love the imagery of a bold blind man walking toward the voice of Jesus!

> And Jesus said to him, "What do you want me to do for you?" And the blind man said to him, "Rabbi, let me recover my sight." (v. 51)

Have you ever wondered why Jesus asked blind people what they wanted? I have. My best guess is that Jesus engaged with them to model how he wants to engage with us. This means he will ask us questions that he already knows the answer to. These conversations help us to focus on who he is and what we actually need. Scripture is clear that we *have* not because we *ask* not. Each blind man who asked was healed, but their healings happened in different ways. Jesus laid hands on some of the blind men, he spit on another man before laying hands on him, and then there was the one who got mud on his eyes that he had to wash off. But the recovery of sight was completely different for Bartimaeus.

> And Jesus said to him, "Go your way; your faith has made you well." And immediately he *recovered his sight* and *followed him* on the way. (v. 52)

Not only did Bartimaeus recover his sight but he also found the One worthy of his focus. Even though Jesus sent him on his way, Bartimaeus had no reason to go back. He'd made his decision when he left behind his beggar's cloak. He was going to move forward as a follower of Jesus.

Bartimaeus wasn't a distraction; he was a divine interruption. Removing blinders of every kind has always been Jesus's focus.

> The Spirit of the Lord is upon me,
>> because he has anointed me
>> to proclaim good news to the poor.
> He has sent me to proclaim liberty to the captives
>> and recovering of sight to the blind,
>> to set at liberty those who are oppressed,
> to proclaim the year of the Lord's favor.
>> (Luke 4:18–19)

Hear me, dearest goddaughter. I believe there is an invitation in this moment. I challenge you not to move forward too quickly and miss it. This is a pregnant pause. Is there an area where life has wrapped you in rags and told you that you shouldn't believe, ask, or even look for more? Cry out. Lift your voice. Stop listening to the dissenting voices that would tell you not to. For too long, women have listened when voices in the crowd told us to.

> *Be silent!*
> *Be busy!*
> *Don't focus . . . multitask!*
> *Be troubled with and distracted by nonessentials.*
> *Attempt everything so that you master nothing.*
> *Interact and listen to the crowd, but don't trouble the master.*
> *Lower your voice rather than raise it.*

I dare you to believe that you can rise above this noise. No one can keep you bound without your permission. There comes significant moments in time when we have to deny the crowd and cry out louder. In this moment I wish I could take you by the hand and whisper,

"Goddaughter, take heart. Get up; he is calling you."

Jesus is waiting. Throw off the cloak of confusion. In his presence you will find clarity. Throw off that beggar's shroud for there is a royal robe of righteousness underneath it. Throw off the "what-ifs" and take heart. He is waiting for you to move forward in his direction. Jesus is calling you out of the crowd to refocus your life. Let's pray.

Heavenly Father,
Have mercy on our areas of crazy confusion, senseless comparison, and ceaseless distractions. This day I choose Jesus as my focus. Help me to find ways that I can make my world more intimate and effective. Reveal any blindness or blindspots and restore my sight. I want to notice the things that truly matter. I want your focus to be mine. Open the eyes of my understanding so I can discern the difference between distractions and God interruptions. In Jesus's name,
Your Daughter

Godmother Conversation Starters

What are some ways you could make your world smaller?

What is distracting you from what you should be focused on?

Who and what should have permission to interrupt you?

Eight

The Balancing Act

Learn from the mistakes of others. You can't live long enough to make them all yourself.

—Eleanor Roosevelt

I am giving you many of my mistakes for your benefit in this chapter. You're welcome. This chapter is going to look and feel a bit different than the other ones. For the record, in addition to being a godmother, I am a mob mom, which loosely translates to a mother of boys. Of course, now mine have all grown into men, so my title reverted back M.O.M., or mother of men, and they have given me the grandest mother title of G-Mama (grandmother). Being a mother has been the most rewarding, empowering, and challenging role of my life. There is nothing I've loved being more, and outside of marriage quite possibly nothing I have made more mistakes in. My hope for this chapter is that you will discover the answers I had to make up along the way.

Not long ago, Heather, one of our all-time favorite babysitters, tagged me in a photo she had taken decades ago. In it, John and I are seated in front of a fountain, surrounded by our three oldest sons. The boys are adorable. I'm guessing Addison was seven, Austin was four, and Alec was two. John looks confident and handsome. I look exhausted.

We were in Hawaii on a layover on our way home from Indonesia. Our first flight was an overnight from Indonesia to Guam. We landed at zero dark thirty, and then the six of us crammed into a single hotel room, pulled the curtains, and slept until the sun came up. As soon as the pool was open, we swam the children to the point of utter exhaustion so they would sleep during our next overnight flight.

We boarded the plane in Guam late that night, and after a full day in the sun I should have fallen asleep immediately, but I didn't. It was back in the days when people smoked on international flights, and I couldn't stop coughing. After hours of restless tossing, I finally dozed off, only to be awakened by a flight attendant shaking my shoulder.

"Are those your children in the row behind you?" I could tell he was not happy. I wanted to say no.

"Yes," I answered without turning around.

"One of them just released the air masks for the entire row."

I flipped around and, sure enough, the babysitter was sound asleep, but Austin was wide awake. Apparently, the masks can be released by a four-year-old armed with a swizzle stick. The flight attendant went on to explain, "This is a completely full flight. It's lucky for you that we are closer to Hawaii than to Guam because, if not, we would have to turn around."

I assumed that he meant lucky as in it wouldn't be necessary to kick us off the plane. Needless to say, I didn't fall back to sleep.

Once in Hawaii, we all crammed into another hotel room and walked the few blocks to the beach, where we repeated the ritual of swimming the children to the point of exhaustion. Later that night, we wandered onto the grounds of the Hilton Hawaiian Village. It was a magical combination of tiki lights, giant koi, Hawaiian music, fire dancers, and penguins! We floated in and out of the brightly lit stores, before we posed for the photo.

In it, two of the boys are rocking amazing mullets, and the other one's golden hair is styled into a bowl cut. (Sorry, guys!) I'm wearing a headband in a failed attempt to control my wayward bangs, which have escaped and shrunk to half their length in the Hawaiian humidity. When I look at the photo, I smile, even though in the picture I am *not* smiling, and I remember why. I was annoyed that my picture was being taken. I was too conscious of my wayward hair, tired face, and false eye.

I'm so happy I didn't get my way that night.

I only wish I could go back to that night, pull my thirty-four-year-old self aside, and have a little talk with her. I would hand over the boys she so often hid behind to either John or the babysitter and draw the young Lisa away for a little chat.

We'd walk quietly until she saw all the beauty that surrounded her in that moment. I would listen for the sigh that signaled that she was relaxed. Then I'd put my hands on her shoulders and look her in the eye and tell her a few things:

Lisa, listen to me, you're doing better than you know. Yes, you've made mistakes and you will make more, but the day is coming when you will realize that God's grace for your children is bigger than your mess-ups. He will redeem your motherhood flaws. Even the worst of your flaws will serve to help your boys to turn to the flawless One.

I know you love being a mother. I know you think it is the only thing you are even marginally good at, so you throw yourself, body and soul, into it. But hear me: it's okay to take care of yourself. There is a vast difference between denying yourself and neglecting yourself. Taking care of yourself is part of loving your children. Neglecting yourself will be counterproductive in the long run. You're imagining that it is a form of self-sacrifice, but it is not. It is self-negligence.

Make time to stretch. A lot of your back pain and problems are due to the fact that your body has carried three children in five years. Stretching will help realign your muscles. And, you're going to need it because if you think three children are a handful, get ready—you're about to have a fourth.

Baby girl, it's time to stop tri-folding your children's underwear. It's time to stop bleaching the white grout on your kitchen floor with a toothbrush. Streamline your life, and let some of the little things go. It is time to get better at playing. Instead of being so quick to pick up what's on the floor, get down on the floor more and play with your boys. Start enjoying your husband and children rather than merely surviving them.

Avoid gossiping women like the plague. They say they want your help, but they really don't. You will hear things you don't want to know, and then in the future, their words will act like a virus and keep you from hearing what you do need to know. Instead of listening to words that steal your strength, lean into God's Word. It is alive and will equip you with the wisdom you need to love your husband, raise your sons, and live generously.

Stop obsessing over what people think about you. A lot of them haven't given you a thought in weeks. This doesn't mean that you are unimportant, it is just that they are too busy with their own issues to even notice how you are navigating yours. Which leads me to another point. Stop investing in relationships with people who don't even want to be your friend. Sweetheart, you need to hear this; they don't like you. It is not because you are unlikable; it is simply because you have so little in common. Don't let it hurt you. Move on because life is too short to do fake friends.

There are some people you just won't click with. That doesn't make either of you wrong. Look at it this way; you know how your sons mixed the pieces from multiple puzzles together only to discover later that the pieces from different puzzles don't fit together? Even if by some crazy chance they are the right shape, they will not create the right picture. You are part of a different puzzle. When the right pieces are in their places, it will be a beautiful picture.

Baby girl, don't force yourself in where you are not wanted— and at the same time, don't hide from what you are meant to be part of. Stop seeing their ambivalence as rejection and accept it as redirection. If you continue to change so that you will fit into their puzzle . . . they will lose respect for you because you were untrue to yourself and neglected developing your unique role and contribution. If this pattern continues, you are not going to like the person you pretend to be. It's time to be honest even if it is more difficult. None of the women you are so desperately trying to befriend at this time will even be in your future because you are going to move away.

Love your husband—I mean really love him. He needs you. Enjoy him and stop acting like a martyr. Both of you will grow more in love as you behave in loving ways. Go for walks, and hire a babysitter for more date nights. Three times a year is not enough. Vacations do not always have to include a time of ministry. Stay home and do a staycation if that is the only way he can take a break. Even though you are tired, make sex a high priority. It is good for both of you. Enjoy that thirty-four-year-old body while you've still got it.

The telephone will steal your time. Develop the habit of not answering your phone now, because the day will come when you will be more connected to a phone than you imagined possible!

Stop worrying about money and the fact that you don't have any health insurance. The money will be there when you need it. Rather than thinking of what you don't have, thank God for what you do have, and you will discover you have more than you know. Develop a habit of generosity with every area of your life. Give as much as you can whenever you have an opportunity.

You are stronger than you know. Hike, surf, and ski. (But don't buy the Ninja motorcycle; that will be a mistake.) And by the way, you are going to shatter your nose for the third time, this time while surfing. When the doctor offers to fix it so that you don't look like a boxer in the future, let him! (I didn't do it because I was afraid of what others might think!) Nobody cares.

P.S. There will be an invention called a flat iron. Watch for it, and when it is available, buy two. Keep one at home, and put the other one in your suitcase. You won't believe the difference it will make in your hair. When this happens, you can stop wearing the headbands that give you headaches.

And there you have it. If only I'd had someone in that season to share with me what I've shared with you, hopefully I would have listened. I know some of this was silly, but a lot of these were lessons I learned the hard way with far more tears than I can count. Especially the one that involved compromising who I was in order to be with people who didn't want to be my friends. I've had a few seasons of God-induced time-outs to help cure me of this pattern. These seasons were painful and redemptive but possibly avoidable. Please feel free to learn from my mistakes.

Recently, I opened up my social media to field questions from young moms. There were so many honest, vulnerable questions from so many sweet young moms wanting to know that this crazy season they are in will count for something. (I promise it *will*!) Many were worried they were not praying or reading their Bible enough, and they wondered if their heavenly Father was less than pleased with them. Please hear my words. In so many ways, *being a mother is living the Bible*. Your heavenly Father has entrusted you with the greatest treasure there is on earth . . . *children*.

Lovely goddaughter, you are not a failure, and you are not missing out. Put on worship music, dance, and sing! There is no *greater privilege*. Be encouraged, young mommies; this is a good season that will position you to go from strength to strength! Here are a few things that will help: It's okay to nap, it's okay to ask for help. It's okay to have a less-than-perfect house! Whatever mommy error you're stressing about . . . it's okay!

Take a deep breath, laugh at your future, and enjoy today.

On these pages, I would like to tackle some of the questions I've received from precious goddaughters on marriage, ministry, and motherhood. Ministry is what my work world looks like, but I believe much

Take a deep breath, laugh at your future, and enjoy today.

of it is translatable to employment in general. Ministry, counseling, and medical professionals, etc., may all feel like the lines between personal and professional get constantly blurred, so I hope this helps.

How do you stay connected to your spouse when you have young kids, and everything is so busy?

Set a bedtime for your children and stick to it. Growing children need more sleep than adults, and adult couples need to set aside time together to grow their relationship. If the goal is to have your children in bed by 8:00 p.m., I'm guessing the process needs to begin no later than 7:00 p.m. This pretty much always fell to me because John traveled, but if you can, divide and conquer the bedtime tasks. Our bedtime ritual included baths, reading a book, singing songs, saying prayers, then going to bed. If you can, have dinner early enough so that your family has plenty of quality time together around the table, with time to spare for games or homework, without having to borrow it from your time together as a couple.

What advice would you give me as a wife of an unbeliever and the sole spiritual leader of the home?

I'd rather you saw yourself as a gateway for God's love to infiltrate your home. Feeling the pressure to spiritually lead others who are not following Jesus means you're probably going to be frustrated. It may help to change your perception of what it means to be a leader. In the kingdom of Christ, leaders are servants. This means we lead best by serving those around us. We invite others to follow Jesus by leading with the example of our lives. Jesus leads us all with love. Don't come under the pressure to change your husband. It never works out well whether they are believers or not. Rather, love your husband and children. The best possible thing you can do is the same thing any of us can do, and that is be a spiritual example of love. Don't preach with your words; preach with something more powerful and persuasive—your life. Model a life that is Christlike. First Peter 3:1–2 says,

> And now let me speak to the wives. Be devoted to your own husbands, so that even if some of them do not obey the Word of God, your kind conduct may win them over without you saying

a thing. For when they observe your pure, godly life before God, it will impact them deeply. (TPT)

You are probably already touching your spouse in ways you cannot yet measure. Don't allow the enemy to pressure you into *saving your spouse*. That is the Holy Spirit's job. Let it be your kindness that leads them to a space of repentance. The story isn't over, lovely goddaughter, and this burden isn't yours. You didn't mention having children, but I made that assumption; if you have little ones, feel free to pour into them every opportunity that you get. Your husband will watch their lives flourish and be drawn to Christ as well.

How do you keep your marriage strong?

Think of the answer in terms of the way you keep your body strong. We eat healthy and build our strength with exercise. In a marriage, this means you guard what you consume and don't shy away from having hard conversations. Having said this, there was a season when all John and I had were hard conversations . . . and that was hard! Make sure there is laughter and love in your home. Don't allow comparison to rob you. If you see another couple enjoying aspects of their marriage that you haven't developed yet, learn from them. Steer clear of entertainment that even hints of porn, adultery, fornication, or the occult. John and I are both super passionate, so we have learned to fight *for* our marriage rather than just fight *in* it. This means attacking problems that arise rather than attacking one another. We also make quarterly contact with a counselor who helps us have the right tools. (We feel so strongly about this that we have featured his course online.) Another thing that is important is to talk about what you hope your marriage will look like a year from now. Dream together and write it down.

What do you do when you feel like your calling is different than your husband's, but he is the "leader" of the family?

Let's first define the role of a leader. A leader is not the boss who controls everything and changes everyone into their image. Leaders empower those under their care. Husbands are to love and lead their wives into who they really are. This means leading in the same manner that Christ loves and leads the church. The Message says,

> Husbands, go all out in your love for your wives, exactly as Christ did for the church—a love marked by giving, not getting. Christ's love makes the church whole. His words evoke her beauty. Everything he does and says is designed to bring the best out of her. (Eph. 5:25–26)

For decades now, this has been John's goal with me. There were times when we did this dance well and other times when we were tripping over one another's feet. True love and leadership lift people to a higher place and perspective. That said, there is a difference in the purpose of marriage and that of the calling or careers we choose. The purpose of marriage is to make us one, not the same.

The purpose of marriage is to make us one, not the same.

If John were a doctor and I felt called to be a minister, this wouldn't be any more of a conflict in our marriage than if I felt called to be a lawyer. I am making the assumption that because you used the word *calling*, one of you may feel called into the ministry. If so, your husband's role as leader would not block your call to ministry, or his call to the ministry should not override what you do. Unless it is because one of you feels that ministry is the direction for your entire family and the other disagrees. Or if what one of you wants to do in ministry means taking you away from your family. (Gosh, I wish we were having coffee so I knew for sure!)

Marriages should be unified in purpose, but that doesn't mean we must have the same roles. John and I are both ministers, but I am not a minister because John is one; I am a minister because that was the call on my life. If I told John that I felt called to move to India and be a missionary, but he didn't agree, as a couple we believe you go with the no. Then we entrust the situation to God, and if someone needs to change their mind, we believe it will happen.

I do think we need to change how we see ministry. As saints, we are all called to do the work of ministry no matter where we actually work. When my children were young, they were my calling (career) and ministry. I wrote books so my written words could travel for me and I could spend more time at home.

Without knowing both sides of your situation, I want to encourage you that there are things that God puts in our heart in one season that are for our next season. Use this season to prepare and build your marriage, and if it is a calling from God, it will come to fruition at the right time.

How do you help your husband understand you and your heart without frustration on either side?

This one took me a long time to learn. And in all honesty, it is an area where I am still learning. One thing I have discovered for certain is that it works better when the goal is to understand each other rather than to be understood by each other. The best way to see your spouse grow in understanding is to model what understanding looks like. Most males find expressing their feelings more difficult than females do. It doesn't mean they don't have deep feelings. When I listen to truly understand John, he knows it. Early on in my marriage, I listened for ways to make my point rather than to grow in my understanding of John. But the approach of understanding worked a whole lot better than arguing my point, sharing my heart, or trying to teach John how to speak the language of a woman's heart, which was completely foreign to him. While your husband is learning how to understand you, make it your goal to understand him. John doesn't do well when I attack his efforts. But he responds favorably when I explain myself in terms that foster discussion while believing the best of him. An example is, "John, when you do that, it feels this way to me, and I know you don't want that."

Good marriages require us to be lifelong learners. Before I open my mouth, I remind myself that "love is patient and kind" (1 Cor. 13:4). Because it is always easier for me to be neither!

What are the keys to joy and longevity in marriage, motherhood, and ministry?

To preserve your joy, never attach it to something or someone that can be taken away from you. In *The Four Loves*, C. S. Lewis warned, "Don't let your happiness depend on something you may lose."[1] Happiness is dependent on what might happen or has happened, but joy runs deeper. Joy is a daily choice. It is the joy of the Lord that is our strength (Neh. 8:10). Joy is lost when we tie it to our marriage, children, or what is happening on social media, in our nation, at work, or even in ministry. I also have discovered that the quickest way to lose my joy is to complain about my current season or circumstances. As soon as any complaining starts on my part, the grace lifts and I am buried under a landslide of discouragement.

How do you balance your marriage, ministry, and family?

This is easier to do if you don't try to separate them. I am always a wife, always a mother, and always a minister. That's who I am at the grocery store, on an airplane, or on a platform. Our identity is first and foremost God's daughter; this is the relationship that lends strength to everything we do. Everything I do outside my home flows from the strength of the relationships inside it. I don't do well with boxes, but I do believe boundaries are incredibly necessary to maintaining balance. Be careful about allowing ministry to become the most prevalant point in this triangle. Your marriage is your ministry—just ask any minister (husband or wife) who neglected theirs only to realize later their grave error. Your children are your ministry. I hate that I hear far too often that many "ministry" children felt like their parents had time for everyone but them. When this happens, resentment builds up. Have conversations and find creative ways to connect with one another and with your children. Family nights filled with laughter, playing games, and eating together is a great start.

How do you prepare yourself for marriage and motherhood?

This is where a relationship with an older woman proves invaluable. Paul admonished Timothy to study in order to show himself approved in 2 Timothy 2:15. He also told Timothy to follow him as he followed Christ. So, we don't just learn by studying the Word; we learn by following living examples. We are created for connection and conversation. The Bible has examples, but we all need to interact in order to get specific advice on specific issues. I'd begin by praying that God would send you a wise godmother (she doesn't have to be old), then watch for her. Find ways to serve alongside her in both ministry capacity and in her home so that you can learn.

What about divorce and remarriage when a husband has left?

I always turn to 1 Corinthians 7:15 as a guide: "But if the unbelieving partner separates, let it be so. In such cases the brother or sister is not enslaved. God has called you to peace." In my opinion, this verse doesn't refer just to a spouse who refused to believe in Jesus but also to one who refused to believe in the sacredness of the marriage covenant. Adulterers leave their marriages with every act of adultery just as abusers deconstruct their marriages with every act of abuse. Allow God to speak his peace into your situation before you make any decision, but I personally believe you are free to marry again.

I need emotional support to know that I'm not ruining my kids when I make mistakes. Where do I go to find it?

First, there is no such thing as a perfect parent. If you want a list of parents who majorly messed up, the Bible is a great resource. Here's a short list: Adam, Eve, Noah, Abraham, Sarah, Lot, Isaac, Rachel, Rebekah, Jacob, Moses, Zipporah, Eli, Samuel, Bathsheba, Jesse, Saul, David, Solomon.

As you know, Jesus came from the lineage of a number of these flawed parents. So, lovely mama, take a deep breath and drop all the false imagery of comparison that is accusing you right now. Guilt is not a good guide, and fear is a horrible counselor.

I know I was hard on my mother, and I was totally convinced I would never make any of her same mistakes, but I did. There came a point when I forgave my mother and father. When I stopped blaming them, I was ready to forgive myself. This interchange will position you to learn from your mistakes, confess your struggles, and receive God's mercy. Don't make the mistake I made of not forgiving myself until I felt that I had sufficiently paid for my own mommy sins. Moms need mercy too. So don't be afraid to humble yourself so the cycle of guilt doesn't continue. Again, there is wisdom to be gathered from the older women in your world.

Moms need mercy too.

One of the most important things in parenting is consistency. When I was growing up, my parents were very unpredictable. I might be grounded for not eating my oatmeal but excused for missing my curfew. My father was a strict disciplinarian one moment and drunk the next. It is very important that your children know what to expect from you. You can't be overly strict one day, then act like you're simply BFFs the next. You can't underparent today because you overdid it yesterday. Own your mistakes. If you were too harsh, confess it. Ask your children for forgiveness. Forgive yourself and begin again. Figure out what is important (character and safety are two good areas to start with) and what isn't (a messy room, hair, or clothing) then be consistent with the major things and more lenient with the minor ones.

I will go a bit further; there are no perfect parenting methodologies. This may not be what you wanted to hear, but it is some of the best emotional support I can offer you. Good parenting will always utilize the same ingredients, but the formula may vary from child to child. I discovered that what worked for my first son did not work for my second son, and what worked for my second and first sons most certainly did not translate well to my third son. By the time I had my fourth, I felt I'd made every mistake possible. I just kept Arden close to make sure the other three boys didn't injure him!

When I raised my sons, there were quite a few complex parenting curriculums that were popular. I was gifted one of them. In all honesty, I was utterly exhausted just reading the instructions. It was so extensive, it felt like a child's version of the book of Deuteronomy. I knew I'd be failing the program more often than my children. I didn't want to build a house of laws; I wanted to construct a home of love and grace. I gifted it to someone else who would understand how to use it.

We love our children and want to do everything right, but this doesn't mean we won't fail. In most cases, this disconnect isn't due to a lack of effort or godliness. We fail because it is not possible for desperately imperfect people to parent perfectly. We need a perfect example to follow. Through the Scriptures, we see how the Father loved this broken world through his Son. Leaning into Jesus and regularly experiencing both his love and his mercy are really the only ways any of us can redeem our mistakes of yesterday.

How do I find a community of other young mothers who are going through the same things I am?

Communities form around what we value. So many young mothers feel isolated, devalued, ill-equipped, and understandably exhausted. They feel a glaring lack of support on multiple levels. These needs span from emotional to cultural and from physical to financial support. Most mothers feel guilty no matter what they do because they are constantly sent the message that it is never enough.

Whenever possible, it is best to garner advice from someone who has already run the race that you now find yourself in. In this case, you don't need a teammate as much as you need a trainer. Someone in the same season you're in will do a great job lending empathy, but understanding can only take you so far. To move forward, you will need tools and the knowledge of how to use them. It's ideal to have access to someone who is on the other side of our struggle and who can act as a guide. Older mama guides, or godmothers, possess the winning combination of insight and experience. When it comes to children, I'd be hesitant to take advice from someone who hasn't experienced their offspring as adults. Until adulthood is reached, parenting is more of a theory than a proof.

I want to challenge this idea of gathering only with young mothers who are *going through the same things* you are. They are great to laugh with, and it's encouraging to know you are not alone. I would suggest inviting at least one godmother into the mix. The insights of someone who is already on the other side of parenting are invaluable. Of course, gathering with people in the same season of life is better than remaining in isolation, but it may be more helpful to include women in their next season who are ready to reach back. I know that literally thousands of young mothers have gathered and watched Moms of Men, a video course I created with my good friend Havilah, which makes me the honorary older woman in the mix.

> *Until adulthood is reached, parenting is more of a theory than a proof.*

This learning gap is one of the vulnerabilities created by the generation gap between literal and figurative mothers and daughters. The younger women have some desperate needs and the older women feel like no one wants what they have to offer. Both sets of women are going to have to wake up and see that this is not helpful. The young women need to be courageous enough to ask for help, and the older women need to be brave enough to offer it. You don't have to know everything to offer something.

Where do I find someone who's been there before to pour into me?

Look around at the grocery stores and coffee shops. Reach out to someone who looks like they are in your next season. I would hope that you could find women in your local church who are deep wells of wisdom and experience. Pray and ask the Holy Spirit where you should look, and then watch for them. There may be just such a woman down the street from you in your neighborhood, or what about a senior living center? I can only imagine there is a plethora of women who think no one wants the treasury of hard-won wisdom that's in their lives. And until you find her, it is my privilege to be your paper godmother.

> You don't have to know everything to offer something.

How do I find time for self-care and time with God?

I believe self-care and time with God are one and the same. Spending time with the One who made me is one of the best ways to care for myself. If I take the dog for a walk, it will refresh my soul and be an opportunity to spend time with God. It won't be a Bible study, but it will be a study of the wonder of creation. Exercise is one of the best ways to care for yourself. A walk or a bike ride invigorates my body and fills my mind with fresh ideas. When I am in barre class, I'm exercising but it's not refreshing. I am sure a measure of both is best, but if you have to choose between an exercise class or a walk in nature, take the walk.

There are usually ways to find the time you need hidden within your day. One way to discover where you have pockets of time would be to take notes on how your time is spent over the course of the next few days. Time can be lost on the phone or attempting to run errands with kids. Look into having groceries delivered. Planned meals save a lot of time. I always keep on hand what I need for a fifteen-minute go-to meal.

Exhaustion will rob your time of strength, productivity, and joy. Staying up late occasionally is okay, but if it becomes a habit, you will notice the night owl devours the early bird who is trying to find the worm. Look for ways you can flip the narrative so you are running your day rather than it running you. When it comes to certain types of work, I'm more productive at night than I am in the early hours. When my boys were really young, I gave myself permission to read my Bible at night because, between getting them off to school and my *slow* wake-up process, morning routines were epic failures.

On some days, your self-care might look like taking a shower . . . alone . . . while listening to worship music. On other days, self-care might mean reading a book for fifteen minutes out in the sunshine. With littles, you will have a better chance of finding bites of time throughout your day rather than hoping for a big chunk. But these brief moments of reprieve can yield big returns in peace. Watch for the portholes of time rather than waiting for large windows to open. And please don't allow self-care to become another item to check off on your list. Because as soon as you make it one, it ceases to be caring.

How do you create silence in the loudness of family life?

Outside of a shower and time alone in my car, I gave up on silence. I found it helpful to cultivate an atmosphere of worship in my house rather than simply noise. I played worship music of some sort almost as soon as we were all up. The songs helped me follow the directive of Paul:

> Let the word of Christ dwell in you richly, teaching and admonishing one another in all wisdom, singing psalms and hymns and spiritual songs, with thankfulness in your hearts to God. (Col. 3:16)

My boys told me they remember the music always playing and me singing and sometimes dancing, and at other times they saw me facedown on the carpet. I'm pretty sure I was praying, "Father, please put a watch over my mouth and give me patience! Let me be slow to speak, quick to listen, and slow to anger!"

This prayer was pretty much a constant refrain in my life. Before you know it, they will all be at school and you will rediscover the sound of silence.

I am a single mom of four boys who works full time—how do I lead them to God?

I would argue that you are a hero and possibly a saint rather than a single mom! Women can lead boys to God just as easily as men can. The power of the gospel is never diminished or increased by the gender that shares it. Just continue to be an example of what a godly mother is: someone who does her best and doesn't make excuses. Baby girl, you are not responsible to fill the gap their father left behind. Just be that mother. The boys will naturally long for a father, and when they do, point them to *the* Father. If you ask my sons, most of them will tell you that even though they heard John preach *in churches* more, they learned as much or more from me at home. And, god-daughter, I am going to believe a godparent will come across your path to love on those boys and help you!

How did you survive the toddler stage?

Toddlers are hilarious. They love pushing the limits, but don't let them push your buttons. I watch my daughter-in-law Juli-anna as she interacts with her toddlers, and she just stays calm. I, on the other hand, distinctly remember screaming in my car at a stoplight because all my boys were crying. It helps to be consistent with discipline and directives. Toddlers are smarter and more capable of cleaning up and potty training than you might suspect. Keep your tone even unless they are in danger and there is reason to raise your voice. Weathering toddler days requires creativity and a sense of humor. Naps are important . . . for both of you. Let the little things go, and focus on training them.

How would you love on your child if they told you they were gay?

This question may contain the answer within it. I would love them as my child. God loves us regardless of our choices. Love and kindness are not endorsements; they are the very things God uses to lead us back to his heart. We can do no less.

How do we deal with shame as mothers when we fail?

I repented, received God's forgiveness, and asked my children to forgive me. God has used some of my worst moments of parenting as a catalyst for healing the pain of others. When we fail as parents, the best thing we can do is be honest, and one of the worst things we can do is make excuses or blame our bad behavior on our children. John and I were far from perfect parents, but the one thing we did well was own our mistakes.

Looking back, I'm pretty sure I made mistakes on a daily basis. I'd call a mom friend, and she would share that she was wrestling with the same thing. It was comforting to know I was not alone, but this knowledge didn't bring any course correction.

There was one particular time when I found myself so frustrated and angry with one of my sons that I was on the verge of hurting him. I saw the terror in his eyes and realized I was about to repeat the same scenario I grew up in and swore I would never do. It was a wake-up call and a catalyst for me to deal with the abuse from my childhood.

What is something you would change about how you mothered your kids in the early years?

I would have been more patient and played with them more.

What were your greatest concerns for your sons as they grew older?

There were years when John traveled so much that he was rarely there for our sons. When he was home, we got him at his worst because he had already given everyone else his best. My oldest son was a young teen and very upset that his father wasn't there for him. I called one of our dear friends for advice. He asked if Addison wanted to marry. A bit confused, I answered, "Yes."

"Okay. Tell Addison that means he will be processing the rest of his life with a woman. He is just getting a head start now."

His words were a gift to both me and my son. And that is just what Addison is doing now with his lovely wife, Julianna.

This is why we need each other. When someone is on our side, we can stand up against any assault. I have had to face some hard things over the past few years, and just knowing I had praying women lifting me up made all the difference. Together, with the Holy Spirit, we have the strength we need for the days ahead.

Godmother Conversation Starters

What are a few of the things that you would say to your younger self?

Capture them here:

What are pieces of advice that could be immediately applied in your life?

Nine

When Our Fairy Tales
Go Awry

We have come from God, and inevitably the myths woven by us, though they contain error, will also reflect a splintered fragment of the true light, the eternal truth that is with God. Indeed only by myth-making, only by becoming "sub-creator" and inventing stories, can Man aspire to the state of perfection that he knew before the Fall.

—J. R. R. Tolkien

Even though fairy godmothers aren't real, the tale of Cinderella is almost universally told. Scholars say there are anywhere between 340 and 3,000 versions! This makes Cinderella *more* than a fairy tale; it is a myth. It has risen to the rank of an archetype, becoming a story with a pattern we all recognize.

Interestingly, the first recorded version of Cinderella is from ninth-century China. In this tale, the heroine, Yeh-Shen, is granted a wish. She is splendidly outfitted to attend the spring festival, and the final detail is a pair of magic golden slippers. The king sees her and is captivated by her beauty. Her evil stepmother sees Yeh-Shen as well, and in true Cinderella form, Yeh-Shen loses one slipper as she escapes. The villagers find it and bring the golden slipper to the king. The king searches until he finds Yeh-Shen. When she puts on the slipper, she is transformed and the king proposes. In this version, the evil stepmother and stepsister are severely punished for their cruelty. They are stoned by the local villagers . . . super intense.

In addition to the Chinese and our Disney version, there are Cinderella stories from these countries: North American Native, Africa, Ireland, Germany, France, Italy, Norway, Greece, Scotland, Bulgaria, Portugal, and England.[1] I believe there is a very specific reason why the story has such a universal appeal.

Let's probe a bit deeper to discover it. What is the first image that comes to mind when you hear the name Cinderella? Is it a glass slipper? A beautiful gown? A wicked stepmother? An abused girl? A rescuing prince? Mean stepsisters? Magic? Or a fairy godmother?

What about redemption? Believe it or not, Cinderella follows the story-arc pattern of "rise, fall, then rise," which author Kurt Vonnegut proposed looks remarkably like another one we are all familiar with:

"Those steps at the beginning look like the creation myth of virtually every society on earth. And then I saw that the stroke of midnight looked exactly like the unique creation myth in the Old Testament." Cinderella's curfew was . . . a mirror-image downfall to Adam and Eve's ejection from the Garden of Eden. "And then I saw the rise to bliss at the end was identical with the expectation of redemption as expressed in primitive Christianity. The tales were identical."[2]

Rather than *myth* and *primitive*, I'd use the words *story* and *origin*. Stories such as Cinderella express longings that are woven so deep within us that we often don't have the capacity to express them in words. And yet, when we hear these stories, they resonate and awaken something dormant within us.

Fairy tale does not deny the existence of sorrow and failure: the possibility of these is necessary to the joy of deliverance. It denies (in the face of much evidence, if you will) universal final defeat . . . giving a fleeting glimpse of Joy; Joy beyond the walls of the world, poignant as grief.

J. R. R. Tolkien[3]

We want to know there is hope, that good will triumph, and tears will be wiped away. We want to believe that death and defeat will be swallowed up in a victory so complete that wickedness and pain will be but the shadow of a memory.

> *We want to know there is hope, that good will triumph, and tears will be wiped away.*

Because Cinderella presents just such a redemptive pattern, let's examine its individual components a bit closer in the hope of adopting some wisdom and insight for the challenges of our day. At this point, I want to look for more of the God factor and less of the fairy. There are some constants in the story, no matter which version you read.

First, Cinderella's father is deceased, emotionally absent, negligent, or powerless. Much like the father in Snow White, he has yielded his power to someone (the evil stepmother) or something. Because of this weakness or loss, Cinderella's father can no longer protect or provide for her, and cruelty and injustice flourish unchecked.

Cinderella is a motherless daughter, oppressed, rejected, and often demoted to a slave in her own household. She is displaced, and those who could be kind to her choose to be mean instead. For the most part, this domination is at the hands of an evil stepmother and her daughter or daughters. There is a tale that involves jealous older sisters who do the harassing and one in which the grandfather oppresses his orphan granddaughter. But in most of the stories, it is an evil stepmother.

The evil stepmother is the antithesis of all things motherhood. There is nothing nurturing or protective about her; she is ambitious and cruel to the extreme. Though this fairy tale makes motherhood an issue of biology, motherhood is an issue of the heart. There are amazing stepmoms who love and care for their stepchildren as if they were their own; they are mothers in every sense of the word. True mothers, whether adoptive, step, or by birth, want their sons and daughters to grow and flourish. Everything in their life works toward the goal of seeing their children go further than they have gone. *Conversely, evil* stepmothers (and the emphasis is on evil here!) use their children to further their own agendas. Even though the evil stepmother means to harm Cinderella, she actually becomes an agent of her transformation. Cinderella has always been outwardly beautiful, but her response to mistreatment weaves a deep and abiding inner strength that surpasses even her beauty.

Cinderella is always portrayed as a raggedy outlier whose outward appearance of poverty betrays her wealth of spirit.

She is consistently kind and selfless in contrast with her step-sisters and stepmother, who are self-centered, unkind, and at times cruel. Cinderella dreams of more, but she is not willing to become like them to get it.

In the many stories, if Cinderella has special slippers, she manages to leave one behind. These slippers are crafted from various materials considered unique or valuable in the story's culture; they are magically shaped from gold and glass or woven from silk and fur.

In each tale, Cinderella rises from the ashes of despair to a position of influence. In some tales, she wins the love of a prince; in others, it is the love of a king; and in a few, Cinderella becomes her own hero. In every tale, it is her goodness, innocence, and compassion that are rewarded.

For the sake of simplifying the telling, I'm going to stay with the Western version that most of us are familiar with. Due to the death of her mother, Cinderella's father has remarried. It is not long before Cinderella becomes the slave of her wicked stepmother and her two stepsisters. She is pushed away from any semblance of family and treated worse than a servant. She is worked to the point of exhaustion by day and sits fireside in ash for warmth by night, thus the name Cinderella. Her spirit remains unbroken as she refuses to allow cruelty to taint her. She is consistently kind to all.

Time passes and a royal ball is thrown for the prince so that he might find his bride. All the women of the kingdom are invited, but Cinderella is forbidden to go. Her stepsisters mock the very idea of Cinderella imagining that she might attend the ball. Even so, she makes her sisters look as beautiful as possible, knowing she'll be left behind.

She doesn't complain in their presence.

She doesn't make them look ugly.

She doesn't say it isn't fair.

She doesn't rob their joy.

She serves them.

When she thinks she's alone . . . she weeps.

And this is when everything changes.

Her fairy godmother enters the story and transforms Cinderella's ordinary into the extraordinary. A pumpkin becomes a gilded carriage, six mice become handsome horses, a large rat a kind coach driver, and common lizards are transformed into splendidly dressed footmen.

Everything is ready, but our girl has nothing to wear. With a touch of her wand, the godmother changes Cinderella's rags into a gown of splendor. And of course, who could forget the sparkling glass slippers? Overwhelmed by excitement, Cinderella boards the carriage. But before she leaves, her fairy godmother warns her that at midnight everything will go back to what it was, and the magic will be lost.

Cinderella loses track of both time and a slipper, which the prince finds. A search is launched; the prince is determined to marry the one who fits the glass slipper. Cinderella is the perfect fit. The fairy godmother returns and dresses her goddaughter even more magnificently than before. The stepsisters realize their grievous mistake, fall at her feet, and beg her forgiveness. Cinderella freely forgives them, finds men of the court for them to marry, and it goes without saying that she and the prince marry and live happily ever after. The author of the French version, Charles Perrault, ends his Cinderella story with a moral: "The fairies' gift of greatest worth is grace of bearing, not high birth. Without this gift we'll miss the prize; possession gives us wings to rise."

Brave goddaughter, don't miss the fact that the extraordinary hides within how we handle the ordinary.

This is the very thing that Paul tells us:

So here's what I want you to do, God helping you: Take your everyday, ordinary life—your sleeping, eating, going-to-work, and walking-around life—and place it before God as an offering. Embracing what God does for you is the best thing you can do for him. (Rom. 12:1 MSG)

God isn't asking us for the extraordinary—that's what he does. He asks for our ordinary. As we are faithful with what others might call mundane, the extraordinary happens. Don't be confused by the ways of the stepmother and stepsisters. They neglected the ordinary in pursuit of the extraordinary. There is treasure in your day to day.

Brave goddaughter, don't miss the fact that the extraordinary hides within how we handle the ordinary.

We'll never go wrong being kind. Cinderella was well on her way to becoming a princess long before she married the prince. Let's learn from her; every gracious response and act of kindness became another layer of adornment. The fairy godmother's wand merely revealed the gown that Cinderella had been weaving through her consistent benevolence and warmth. These are the choices that give us . . .

Wings to rise above pettiness.

Wings to rise above jealousy.

Wings to rise above mistreatment and tragedy, and finish well.

Adversity was the wind that taught her to fly.

Even when we are treated like rejected stepdaughters, we have the power to respond like daughters of a King. I think we love the story of Cinderella because long ago we were invited to a royal celebration that will begin our happily ever after. Even now, your garment is being woven and your place is being set. The Prince has found you and thrown wide the doors of welcome.

> Let us rejoice and exalt him and give him glory,
>> because the wedding celebration of the Lamb
>> has come.
> And his bride has made herself ready.
> Fine linen, shining bright and clear,
>> has been given to her to wear,
>> and the fine linen represents
>> the righteous deeds of his holy believers.
>> (Rev. 19:7–8 TPT)

It is the Lord who clothes us and his righteousness that robes us. I think it is fair to say that his godliness wove our gown.

And now let's talk a bit more about the role of this marvelous slipper. The slipper was the *tangible* item that set Cinderella apart from all the other women in the room. It was the physical item that represented the hidden loveliness of her spirit. The slipper was something uniquely crafted for and gifted to her. There wasn't another young woman in the room who had what she had and no one else could wear her slipper or take it away. This revelation gave Cinderella a sense of undisturbed peace when all the other ladies in the kingdom were trying it on.

The slipper was the only item of her outfit that did not change back to its original form. Maybe Cinderella was barefoot when her fairy godmother showed up, or maybe the slipper just reflected her walk, which was always consistently golden and transparent. Whatever the reason, the slipper became her identifier. It was the homing device that led the prince back to her. The two were inseparable; Cinderella and her slipper were one and the same in the mind of her royal suitor. He knew that where he found the owner of the slipper, he would find his bride.

The slipper was the symbol or signet that there was more to our legend lady than what met the eye. To explain, I will reach back to the days of my high school French. There is a French phrase that every woman should live, even if she finds it difficult to pronounce. The words are *je ne sais quoi*. This literally means "I know not what." The phrase is used to describe what is appealing or attractive about someone or something that you find difficult to frame with words. Cinderella had some serious *je ne sais quoi* going on.

In our day, this *I know not what* may be as simple as the increasingly rare commodity known as feminine virtue and kindness. Virtue is best defined as moral excellence. Virtue is the attribute that weaves together all that is just, courageous, ethically superior, honorable, and worthy of merit. The opposite of virtue is cowardice, wickedness, and vice.

Bullies are secretly cowards. Their oppression of others is a form of self-protecting. Driven by fear, they operate in the knowledge of the kingdom of darkness and cannot understand that, ultimately, we rise by lifting

> Virtue is the attribute that weaves together all that is just, courageous, ethically superior, honorable, and worthy of merit.

others and begin to fall as we oppress them. The dark bullying of the evil stepmother only served to highlight the light within Cinderella. The stepmother was the furnace that worked gold into Cinderella's life.

Because Cinderella was good, she did good. In this tale, her virtue expressed itself most obviously in kindness. Kindness acts like a key that unlocks people and circumstances. In the most recent Cinderella movie, her mother told her to "have courage *and* be kind." More and more, it seems it will take courage *to* be kind.

Most of us will never have an actual glass slipper that declares there is something more to us, but all of us can develop virtue and kindness. Because our Prince is all good, we are empowered to do good. We have been sealed with a gift that is holy. Let's behave as such. Because it is confusing when royal daughters act like grasping, competitive stepsisters.

The Holy Spirit is the counselor sent to transform us into who we really are. Let's not grieve the very One who empowers us. Virtue is not something that we slip on and off. This gift cannot be purchased or stolen, and it is greater than any magical blessing a fairy godmother might convey. Our gift comes from our Prince. His gift is alive within us (1 John 2:27). We have a measure of the Prince's Holy Spirit within us. It is our surety of welcome on the other side of this pain.

THE ORIGINAL STORY

If the tale of Cinderella reflects our time in Eden (rise), our tragic midnight banishment (fall), and the redemptive promise of welcome into an eternal kingdom (rise), then let's visit our origins in Genesis in a fairy tale form.

There once was a magnificent immortal prince who reflected the image of his glorious Creator. The Creator's words were alive with power; each sound he breathed formed something out of nothing. The Creator was the all-good Father of Light who long ago banished the shadowed dark angel from his realm.

He planted a garden for the prince, filling it with trees that were beautiful and useful for food. In the center of this orchard stood two trees of power: the tree of life and the tree of the knowledge of good and evil. The Creator warned the prince that the fruit of the tree of knowledge of good and evil would strip him of life and put him under the domain of the shadow of death.

The prince was entrusted with tending this realm of wonder. Each day brought a new revelation of the Creator's goodness. But something was amiss. The prince was lonely. God created a woman to be his companion and co-laborer. She was perfectly like him and yet uniquely different. They lived together in the unspoiled wonder of a realm without death or time.

One day, a serpent approached the man and woman. He shaded the Creator's words until his lies sounded like truth. They ate the fruit, and everything changed.

A veil of light fell from their eyes, and their nakedness became apparent. Shackled by self-consciousness, they wove garments to cover their shame. When they heard the Creator call . . . they hid.

The Creator recognized shadow on his children of light. He knew that, for their sake, they could not remain in the presence of the tree of life. They had to leave.

The serpent was cursed to the lower form of a snake. The earth lost a measure of its fruitfulness; now the man would labor to bring forth the fruit he had once simply tended. But to me, the woman's loss is the most heartbreaking. She will love yet in return be oppressed and ruled, and childbirth will come with multiplied pain. And yet hidden within all that loss, there was a promise.

> I will put enmity between you [the serpent] and the
>   woman,
>   and between your offspring and her offspring;
> he shall bruise your head,
>   and you shall bruise his heel. (Gen. 3:15)

Two things are immediately apparent: the reality of enmity, and the promise of hope on the other side. The day would come when her seed would prevail. Pain was promised, but pain was not the promise. Life was the promise. There was a legacy of hope in her future. In time, the shadow of death would begin to yield to the Prince of Light.

Their dominion had fallen into domination, creation's order was doomed to chaos, and the multiplication of Eden turned into division as endless life bowed to death.

THE PRESENCE OF DRAGONS

It simply isn't an adventure worth telling if there aren't any dragons in it.

Sarah Ban Breathnach [4]

This is a quote I'd rather not have as a reality. But there you have it. Goddaughter, we've been woven into just such an adventure. Long ago, a special war was set in motion between the children of God and a dragon. Even though our tale is ancient, we find the destruction of the dragon today.

Eve left behind a garden serpent, not knowing the day would come when her descendants would face an angry dragon. Time passed. The serpent grew in hatred and became a dragon, and the woman grew into a people of strength called Israel.

In fulfillment of his promise, the Creator sent another Prince. The promised offspring of the woman, God's only begotten Son. The one destined to crush the great serpent's head. Now what about that dragon? Who is it?

The dragon's true name is Satan, once named Lucifer until his pride and greed unmade him. The dragon represents his nature more than his form. He is the ruler of the shadow realm, the father of lies, a thief, murderer, and destroyer. He is the one who accuses (both male and female) in an attempt to shame us into complacency. His language is a web of slander, comparison, competition, distortions, and division with one goal: to deceive. But he is not God's equal. C. S. Lewis explained, "Satan, the leader or dictator of devils, is the opposite, not of God, but of Michael."[5]

As I read the Genesis account and scan the reports of our world, it seems that our world is more broken than ever. Rather than a rise, it feels like we are poised for another midnight tumble. Satan's handiwork surrounds us. We see its shadow in the form of wars, racism, jealousy, greed, selfish ambition, vile and perverse practices, sex trafficking, pornography, misogyny, misandry (the hatred of men), abortion, and occult practices. These and more have flooded our earth in an attempt to overwhelm the people of God.

> The serpent poured water like a river out of his mouth after the woman, to sweep her away with a flood. But the earth came to the help of the woman, and the earth opened its mouth and

swallowed the river that the dragon had poured from his mouth. (Rev. 12:15–16)

The very earth intervenes and averts this destruction because all creation is waiting and watching, desperate for a revelation of God's sons and daughters. Creation knows we are the rightful guardians even if we have forgotten.

> Then the dragon became furious with the woman and went off to make war on the rest of her offspring, on those who keep the commandments of God and hold to the testimony of Jesus. (Rev. 12:17)

The one woman, Eve, became Israel, from whom came a virgin, Mary, who birthed the Christ, who gave birth to his bride on the cross when the second Adam's side was opened up. We are that bride, those who keep his commandments and hold to the testimony of Jesus.

This dragon embodies the antichrist spirit, which hates all the sons and daughters of the Most High God. According to John's vision in Revelation, he does seem to have a special design against women. One of his ploys is to set men and women at odds with one another.

Things are once again not good with Adam and Eve. More and more men are alone and now imagine that alone is better. It could be that these men are hiding from God. It could be that these men are hiding from their future. It could be that these men are hiding from reality. Instead of searching for women who could help them . . . I fear many are hiding from us.

I've sought to empower women for three decades. I long to see women freed from the chains of control so they can know their true value and be loosed from bonds of self-consciousness. I understand that it is important for them to learn how to navigate anger in constructive ways and recover the power of their virtue. I want them to know what it might look like to fight like a girl while being nurturing and rising like a lioness. I want to see women with swords embracing an identity without rival, woven in adamant, immovable truth.

In so many ways and in so many places, this has happened. Women are free to pursue their dreams of education and careers, to which I say, "Well done." They are producing films and heading up companies. They hold seats in government. Women have risen in visibility and influence on every front. We have proven ourselves more than capable. But talent and ability are not multipliers if they lack virtue. God is looking for a bride who is both virtuous and capable. We've experienced a noble rebirth; now he seeks women of noble character. "Who can find a virtuous and capable wife? She is more precious than rubies" (Prov. 31:10 NLT).

> *We've experienced a noble rebirth; now he seeks women of noble character.*

I fear Adam is lost and doesn't know how to find his way back home. We are not to blame, but he needs our help. Yes, there are those who say that the declining state of men is the fault of women. Their theory is that as women rise, men are displaced or replaced. I find this answer far too simplistic. It is always easier to blame than change. I do not agree that the absence of men is the fault of the daughters. This injury runs far deeper.

Adam's sons have not been good to the daughters of Eve. Adam and Eve were once one; therefore, when men mistreat women, they inevitably wound themselves. How long can one oppress others before they find themselves likewise oppressed? There has been far too much abuse of women for far too long. This abuse is not isolated to developing nations; it happens in your neighborhood. Women have been abused in houses of worship as well as in their places of employment.

The rate of fathers neglecting and abandoning their children has soared to alarming levels nationwide, with an estimated 80 percent of all single-parent households led by mothers.[6] When men neglect their families, women have no choice but to rise and meet the need themselves. I believe strong women have the power to make strong men even stronger. Just as I believe that strong men make women stronger. It is the weak in both genders who blame and oppress. I have heard it said that when women act like men, men act like boys. But I wonder if the reverse isn't a truer statement. When men act like boys, women act like men . . . because they feel they have to. Women, who were once downtrodden, have risen. And rising is a good thing.

Having risen, what do we do? Do we mistreat those who mistreated us? We are capable of this as women, but it is not an option if we are virtuous. God wove male and female so intimately that what frees one frees the other. What binds one eventually binds the other. Men wound themselves when they treat what God called good as though it were not. And the same is true for women.

The questions that now need to be answered are, Can we help? Does our original purpose of helpmeet still stand? Is this still part of our destiny? Do we rise as agents of healing to those who have done so much harm to us? Now that we have found our voice—how will we use it? Will it be in wisdom and kindness, or will we limit it to a cry for vengeance? Can what is not good be made good again? I believe God's answer is yes.

Hate will not heal women any more than it has healed men. When people are empowered but not purposed, there is a risk that their power will be misused. The daughters of Eve have found their voices; let's use them to denounce what's wrong, then raise our voices, male and female, to work together to make things right.

The glass slipper was Cinderella's tangible reminder that her transformation had not been a dream. Daughters who wear glass slippers must learn to tread lightly. Let's not stomp our feet in anger and shatter what elevates us. Broken glass is a tricky thing to clean up, and we don't want to leave shards of glass behind that would wound the sons and daughters who follow in our footsteps.

In the struggle for our God-given rights, let's not embrace the wrong.

In the struggle for our God-given rights, let's not embrace the wrong. There is no reason to demand from others what is already ours. It is time to simply walk in it. I found this next passage intriguing:

> How long will you waver,
> O faithless daughter?
> For the LORD has created a new thing on the earth:
> a woman encircles a man. (Jer. 31:22)

All the commentaries I've read agree that the last line is a mystery. One commentary on Jeremiah 31:22 reads, "Rachel's poem closes with an enigmatic line. God promises to the 'faithless daughter' Israel to create 'a new thing on the earth: a woman encompasses a man' (31:22). Literally translated, the second line reads, 'a female surrounds a warrior,' but its meaning for the poem is not clear."[7]

When I close my eyes, I see a seated warrior enfolded in the arms of a woman. She stands behind him, whispering in his ear, reminding him that he is a prince and that dragons are real. She encompasses him to once again remember that together they have the power of dominion to make what is not good . . . good again.

We have a lot of work to do, and it's not going to happen unless we do it together, men and women. But for now, let's start with us. Women should always be advocates for each other but never at the expense of men. Nor at our own expense. Let's open up our feminine treasury and retrieve from it the powerful gift of nurture in order to speak words of life that have the power to build.

Yet we are not of those who are foolish enough to imagine that we can get our value from one another. Our value cannot be stolen by anyone called male or female. Our value comes from a higher source, one both unseen and invincible.

For you were created in the image of God. And he left nothing undone. The second rise in the oldest story on earth has happened. We fell, but he rose. And he's offered us our truest identity in the process:

For we are his workmanship, created in Christ Jesus for good works, which God prepared beforehand, that we should walk in them. (Eph. 2:10)

Godmother Conversation Starters

Do you believe that the mandate for women to help take what is not good (men alone) and make it good still stands?

List some *je ne sais quoi* attributes that you see in the female gender.

What are some ways that women are stomping their feet in glass slippers?

Ten

The Gender Gap

Of all the bad men, religious bad men are the worst.

—C. S. Lewis

I will forever remember the very first time I spoke to a mixed-gender audience. I didn't ask to speak, and I certainly did not want to speak at any gathering, especially one that included males and females. The one who thought this would be a good idea was my husband. I was pregnant with our second son, and John served as a college and career pastor. John was scheduled to go on an outreach trip, which meant he'd miss a Tuesday night service. This had never been a problem in the past because the high school and junior high pastors were always happy to fill in for him.

When he broke the news to me, I begged him to reconsider. I quoted John every Scripture that has ever been used to invalidate women as ministers. I brought up the topic of head coverings, usurping authority, and silent women. John explained that it was impossible for me to usurp his authority if he was the one asking me to speak and the senior pastor had approved it. And as far as the issue of my head being covered and staying silent, he didn't agree with my interpretation. I even asked the high school pastor to speak in my stead, but John had gotten to him first, so he refused. When my husband makes up his mind about something that he believes he's heard from God on, he won't be swayed.

My next step was to defy John. I let him know that my answer was no and that I wouldn't do it. After all, I wasn't on staff, and I had just as much right as anyone else to say no. That is when he backed me into a corner and asked if that was what God was telling me to do.

At the time, I had no idea what God was saying to me! I just knew I was terrified. I knew I had no desire to speak to the group, and I was pretty sure they were great with not hearing from me. The challenging thing was, I felt that in my time of Bible study, God had highlighted a possible passage for me to speak on. But I continued to push back.

Rather than announce who was speaking, John told everyone that there would be a mystery guest in a few weeks. This worked for me because it meant there was still a possibility that I wouldn't have to speak. I was in agony as I wrestled to be able to answer John's question truthfully. I was trying to determine what was worse, refusing my husband or disobeying God.

Finally, I caved. After all, most of the people had been in our youth group for two years. All of them knew me. John recorded a video that was to be played as my announcement before I got up. On the night I was meant to speak, I was in the back . . . sweating. I couldn't help but notice that John's idea of a mystery guest speaker had created quite a bit of interest. This meant we had a lot more visitors in our group than usual. As worship wound down, my whole body was seized with panic. After welcoming everyone, one of our leaders made a few announcements, then hit the play button on the video. There was my husband's handsome face. He was so excited to introduce his favorite speaker.

Then he dropped the bomb that it was his wife. For a moment, you could hear a pin drop. This brief silence was followed by the noise of metal chairs being sharply closed and thrown into the stacking bin. As people exited the room, they glanced my way. Their disapproval was palpable. I heard men and even some women declare that there was no way they were staying to hear a woman. I waited and watched until the last person left and the door was slammed behind them.

As I made my way to the front of the room, there was no missing the fact that the crowd had shrunk by more than half. There were tears in my eyes as I muttered that I wanted to leave as well. Our sweet leaders remained. They did their best to smile, nod, and add their encouragement. Afraid of being in any way unscriptural, I am pretty sure I just read some passages out loud. The entire time I spoke, I heard the very Scriptures that I'd rehearsed earlier to John playing in my mind as accusations.

I suffer a woman not to preach or teach.

Women are to be silent in the church.

Why was my head uncovered?

When service was over, I was surrounded by encouragement. I will always be thankful for their kindness. As soon as I could, I gathered our two-year-old son from the nursery and headed home to put my pregnant self to bed. After I got Addison down, I hurried to get ready myself. Within a few minutes of turning off the light, I heard someone pound on my bedroom window.

I froze. There was a fence around the back of our house, but no actual curtains on our bedroom windows. I was downstairs in the dark, alone and vulnerable. I heard the Holy Spirit whisper, "Turn on the light."

At first, I thought, "No, that will mean they will see me!" I heard, "Let them."

I was shaking, but a measure of courage entered my heart. I jumped out of bed, flipped on the light, picked up the phone, and called the police. Then I flipped on all the outside lights.

I never found out who it was that thought scaring a pregnant woman was a godly countermove to check me for preaching. It all felt very Ku Klux Klanish. I grew up hearing stories of how the Klan used to drive through my father's childhood neighborhood, shooting at the homes of Catholic Italians. The police used their flashlights to show me the shoe prints where my intimidators had climbed back over the fence.

When John returned home, I shared what had happened. He was disappointed to hear that so many people had walked out on me. He was outraged that some guys who called themselves Christians would trespass on his property to frighten his wife. I explained that it was just too hard for me. That the double standard was just too extreme. I assured him that I never wanted to speak to men again. He nodded his agreement, then countered, "I understand, but I can't let you do that, Lisa; there are too many young women watching."

That was more than thirty years ago.

It's time to flip on the lights. The day for cowering in the dark while someone pounds on our bedroom windows is over. I know I am asking you to do the brave, hard thing, and it would be easier if you didn't. Please don't. Our shrinking has not served anyone well.

God's daughters have awakened, and they will no longer be shamed into silence. We are not Bible-ignorant pagan women. We are godly, intelligent, God-fearing women who understand the Bible well enough to recognize bad theology when we hear and see it. The time has come to close the gender gap. If we don't, it will continue to widen, leaving our sons and daughters vulnerable to great risk. Rather than bemoan our gender, I believe it is time to realize what is expressed in it.

Lovely one, please hear me:

Female is beautiful.

Woman is a God-assigned designation and a gift.

Don't for a second imagine that woman was an afterthought. She was always part of creation's divine design.

From the very beginning, God created woman as an answer to be embraced rather than a problem to be controlled.

Male and female are both created in the image of God.

God created men to reflect his glory.

Male and female were woven as a power union.

God wouldn't have given us a voice if he'd intended for us to be silent in the presence of one another.

Our voices should be used to attack the real enemy (Satan, the father of lies) rather than to accuse and attack one another.

We are in a war in which male and female are intimate allies rather than enemies. (But we are treating one another like enemies.)

The enemy divides us in the hope that we will use our strengths against one another.

Our misuse of our God-given dominion weighs heavily on creation, the family, and marriages.

> *God created woman as an answer to be embraced rather than a problem to be controlled.*

THE GENESIS GAP

Even *before* the fall of humankind, there was a gap. The man's vulnerability was discovered amid the wonder of creation.

> Then the LORD God said, "It is not good that the man should be alone; I will make him a helper fit for him." (Gen. 2:18)

It is the first time we see the use of the phrase *not good*. Creation was perfect, God was present, yet someone was absent. It wasn't that something bad was present; it was that something good was missing. My daughter-in-law Juli makes amazing desserts for my husband. If we had a family dinner and Juli forgot the dessert, John would think, *This is not good*. He'd be happy with the food on the table, but the fact that we were missing a dessert would translate to dinner being not good. It would be the situation that was not good. Adam was not bad; the fact that he lacked someone who fit with him was not good.

This man who was created in the image of God had no one who reflected his. To rectify this, God entrusted Adam with naming all the animals.

> Now out of the ground the LORD God had formed every beast of the field and every bird of the heavens and brought them to the man to see what he would call them. And whatever the man called every living creature, that was its name. (Gen. 2:19)

We are so insulated and isolated from the vast majority of creation, I am not even sure we can capture the magnitude and wonder of this parade of animals. Scientists estimate that there are presently 6.5 million species of land animals on the earth. This does not include the over 950,000 insects or all the aquatic life.[1] If Adam took ten seconds to name each animal, then this process would have taken just a little over two years. If the naming process took ten minutes per animal, then it would have been over 123 years as we measure time.

This was no small undertaking, and I don't envision that it was hurried. In order to name something, I'm guessing there would have been interaction. With each of our sons, John and I chose a few name options, but it wasn't until we held them in our arms and looked deep into their eyes that we knew their correct names. Being named is a way of saying something belongs because the name becomes one with its bearer.

And I marvel at how intelligent this first man must have been. The very fact that he could remember so many names is mind boggling.

> The man gave names to all livestock and to the birds of the heavens and to every beast of the field. But for *Adam there was not found a helper fit for him.* (Gen. 2:20)

Imagine what this was like. Adam experienced animal after animal, beast after beast, and bird after bird. He saw that each creature was paired with their perfect other, the one fashioned and fit for them, but for Adam there was none. The encounter with the serpent suggests that Adam and Eve had the ability to interact with the creatures. Adam was guardian and master to all, but the gap—his longing, the breach that was not good— remained. He was missing the key relationship that would unlock his life.

Adam didn't know what he needed; he just knew he needed. As it was for Adam, so it is for us. We all carry an innate awareness that there is something more. Even now, we peer through a temporal haze hoping to catch a reflection of how our Bridegroom sees us. First Corinthians 13:12 describes this dynamic: "For now we see in a mirror dimly, but then face to face. Now I know in part; then I shall know fully, even as I have been fully known."

Adam didn't know what he needed; he just knew he needed.

Gaps and longings, which are deep within us, are never satisfied with something outside of us. Adam needed someone who fit him.

> So the LORD God caused a deep sleep to fall upon the man, and while he slept took one of his ribs and closed up its place with flesh. And the rib that the LORD God had taken from the man he made into a woman and brought her to the man. (Gen. 2:21–22)

The seed of Eve was in the marrow of the man. Science suggests the bone marrow contains stem cells that can be used to regenerate human tissue and organs.[2] Eve was not Adam's clone; she was his most intimate *other*. Like him yet uniquely unlike him. Woman is the beautiful reflection of all man lacks. Together their strength is made perfect. The one (Adam) became two (man and woman) so that the two could become one again.

I want to pull forward some of what I wrote over a decade ago in my book *Fight Like a Girl*: "The differences in our genders were meant to make us one. Just as it was *not good* for Adam to be alone, it was also not good for the woman to remain hidden within the man. Woman was a necessary addition to creation."[3]

FIGHTING BAD THEOLOGY

How has the image of male and female become twisted into an unrecognizable version of its former beauty and strength? There are many answers to this question. Culture and fear have driven us apart. Mean-spirited religion accuses women and places them back under the curse of the fall. Entertainment has made sport of the genders by pitting them against one another. This gender gap goes deep and reaches back to Eden. With that kind of baggage, it's easy to forget that we once were one.

In *How It All Began*, Bob Utley points to Walter Kaiser's assertion that the translation of a helper in Genesis means one who is fit to be "'a power (or strength) corresponding to man' (or equal to man)."[4] If this assertion is correct, it would explain why the woman was co-heir and image bearer and, as such, shared power or dominion over creation with the man. She reflected him in her ability to think and communicate. We know that in most external ways, men are physically stronger than women. This is for men to protect women and children. Yet it is interesting that the strongest muscle in the human body, according to weight, belongs solely to women . . . it is the womb or uterus.

"A laboring uterus exerts incredible pressure to push a baby out into the world, and is the strongest force exerted by any muscle in the body."[5] This is one example of how women are equal in strength but vastly different than men. Differing strength does not mean unequal; it is one of many reasons that male and female help fill in one another's gaps.

In order to remember who we are, we need to fight back the shame that comes along with bad theology. For example, when you read the following interchange, what do you think and feel?

As he said these things, a woman in the crowd raised her voice and said to him, "Blessed is the womb that bore you, and the breasts at which you nursed!" But he said, "Blessed rather are those who hear the word of God and keep it!" (Luke 11:27–28)

Was Jesus shutting her down or correcting this woman for raising her voice? Was he implying that what his mother Mary did was unimportant?

For years I read these verses with hints of all of the above. When you are repeatedly shamed for your gender, that shame will worm its way into how you read Scripture. If you've been taught that women are a problem to be controlled, that is how you will read the passage.

When my feminine soul was healed, I no longer heard the words of Jesus in this passage as an attempt to put a woman in the crowd in her place or silence her. Instead, I heard an invitation. The blessing of obedience is open to all. It is not limited to Mary, the one woman who carried and nursed him . . . it is available to all women who hear the Word of God and keep it. With this one statement, Jesus threw wide the door by telling all women they could be blessed whether they were barren or surrounded with offspring. When we are those women who not only hear the Word but allow it to become alive in us, people are born again. Obedience opens a door to all of us, male and female alike.

Recently, there has been a resurrection of the discussion of head coverings. Now women are wondering if this is a practice that should be adopted in our churches. Some are suggesting that women should pray in beanies or with their hands hovering over their heads as a way of honoring Paul's directive in 1 Corinthians 11.

The issue of head coverings is only brought up to the Corinthian church. We no longer need to be theologians to gain access to their writings. My new friend and big sister Elyse Fitzpatrick pointed me in the direction of an academic book by Dr. Philip B. Payne titled *Man and Woman, One in Christ: An Exegetical and Theological Study of Paul's Letters*. In his work, Dr. Payne explained that in the Greek culture, men traditionally wore their hair short. If a man wore his hair long, it was an invitation to other men for a homosexual liaison. Greek women of good reputation wore their hair up; if a woman wore her hair down, it indicated sexual availability. The Greek culture of Corinth was rife with both homosexuality and promiscuity. In addition to this, men wearing their hair long like women's and women wearing their hair down were in keeping with cult worship in Corinth, whose practices undermined God's plan of marriage. The following is 1 Corinthians 11:4–10 translated from the Greek with Dr. Payne's notes:

> Every man who prays or prophesies with effeminate hair hanging down from his head disgraces himself [lit. his head]. And every woman who prays or prophesies with her hair hanging down loose [lit. head uncovered, the sign of a suspected adulteress] disgraces herself [lit. her head], for she is one and the same with her who is shaved [the punishment of a convicted adulteress]. For if a woman does not do her hair up [lit. cover her head], let her have her hair cut off; but if it is disgraceful for a woman to have her hair cut off or shaved, let her do her hair up [lit. cover her head]. For a man ought not to display effeminate hair [lit. cover his head], since he is the image and glory of God [and so should live in a way that upholds God's design in creation and brings God glory]. The woman [not another man] is the pride and joy of man. For man did not

come from woman, but woman from man [to be his sexual partner]; neither was man created for woman, but woman for man [to be his sexual partner]. On account of this, the woman ought to have control over her hair [lit. head] by doing it up modestly, on account of the angels [who observe worship and report to God].[6]

Because of the angels who are present, we should worship God in a way that honors his creation of male and female. Christians are not to advertise any form of sexual promiscuity, how much more so in worship.

Next, let's read these verses from the Passion Translation (Aramaic), beginning with 1 Corinthians 11:3.

But I want you to understand that Christ is the source of every human alive, and Adam was the source of Eve, and God is the source of the Messiah.

Again, we see the creation order established.

Any man who leads public worship, and prays or prophesies with a shawl hanging down over his head, shows disrespect to his head, which is Christ. And if any woman in a place of leadership within the church prays or prophesies in public with her long hair disheveled, she shows disrespect to her head, which is her husband, for this would be the same as having her head shaved. (1 Cor. 11:4–5 TPT)

Here it becomes very clear that Paul is speaking to those who are visible in some form of influence or leadership. This is not a regulation made for new converts but for those who lead. This passage says men don't need to cover their heads because

Christ is their source, and women who wear their hair down are dishonoring the sanctity of one flesh with promiscuity.

> If a woman who wants to be in leadership will not conform to the customs of what is proper for women, she might as well cut off her hair. But if it's disgraceful for her to have her hair cut off or her head shaved, let her cover her head. (1 Cor. 11:6 TPT)

Again, it was the rebellious women who were invited to cover their heads. I'm reading, wear your hair correctly (up like a respectable Greek woman), or shave it so as not to send mixed signals, and if that's not an option, then cover that head! Then it is back to the creation order again:

> A man in leadership is under no obligation to have his head covered in the public gatherings, because he is the portrait of God and reflects his glory. The woman, on the other hand, reflects the glory of her husband, for man was not created from woman but woman from man. By the same token, the man was not created because the woman needed him; the woman was created because the man needed her. For this reason she should have authority over the head because of the angels. (1 Cor. 11: 7–10 TPT)

N. T. Wright makes this point in his book *Surprised by Scripture*: "[Paul's] main point is that in worship men should follow the dress and hair codes that proclaim them to be male, and women the codes that proclaim them to be female."[7]

Paul returned to addressing the gender inequality gaps:

> So then, I have to insist that in the Lord, neither is woman inferior to man nor is man inferior to woman. For just as woman

was taken from the side of man, in the same way man is taken from the womb of woman. God, as the source of all things, designed it this way. (1 Cor. 11:11–12 TPT)

And closing out the discussion,

So then you can decide for yourselves—is it proper for a woman to pray to God with her hair unbound? Doesn't our long-established cultural tradition teach us that if a man has long hair that is ornamentally arranged it invites disgrace, but if a woman has long hair that is ornamentally arranged it is her glory? This is because long hair is the endowment that God has given her as a head covering. (1 Cor. 11:13–15 TPT)

The Greek men who were fixing their hair ornamentally like the Greek women could be perceived as inviting same-sex involvement from the platform. The conclusion that Dr. Payne comes to after all of this is,

The most important application of this passage today is what Paul stresses in the climax of the passage, that men and women should show respect to each other, honoring the opposite sex as their source. As Paul stresses in the climax of this passage, believers must affirm the equal rights and privileges of women and men in the Lord. Women as well as men may lead in public Christian worship. Since in the Lord woman and man are not separate, women who are gifted and called by God ought to be welcomed into ministry, just as men are.[8]

In summary, if you want to wear a head covering, then wear one, but it is not a requirement for women who profess godliness. What is a requirement is that we do not dress or behave in a way that is seductive and dishonoring of our husbands if we are married, or that undermines the purpose of worship if we are single. I will close with this thought: Do you really think that angels were concerned about a piece of cloth or that in worship our lives honored our Father with holiness rather than the mixed messages of a culture that blended the sexual in their practices of worship?

Another hot topic: What about women preaching? Doesn't 1 Timothy 2:11–15 forbid women from preaching? First, let's read the Scripture:

> They must be allowed to study undisturbed, in full submission to God. I'm not saying that women should teach men, or try to dictate to them; rather, that they should be left undisturbed. Adam was created first, you see, and then Eve; and Adam was not deceived, but the woman was deceived, and fell into trespass. She will, however, be kept safe through the process of childbirth, if she continues in faith, love and holiness with prudence.[9]

In N. T. Wright's book *Paul for Everyone*, the Scripture above is under the heading, "Women Must Be Allowed to Be Learners." What I hear in these verses is Paul instructing Timothy on how to pastor Greek women who were new converts. The apostle Paul is also addressing the fear those women would have had giving birth outside of what they had come to know as the protection of the Temple of Diana. Are we first-century Greek Christians who believe the man came from the woman? Or are we of those who believe that the first woman was born of a man? I am of the second mind. In his explanation, Wright goes on to say,

> Why then does Paul finish off with the explanation about Adam and Eve? Remember that his basic point is to insist that women, too, must be allowed to learn and study as Christians, and not

be kept in unlettered, uneducated boredom and drudgery. Well, the story of Adam and Eve makes the point: look what happened when Eve was deceived. Women need to learn just as much as men do. Adam, after all, sinned quite deliberately; he knew what he was doing, he knew that it was wrong, and he deliberately went ahead. The Old Testament is very stern about that kind of action.[10]

Ignorance of the Scriptures will exact a terrible price on both men and women. The gospel is to be preached by God's sons and daughters! Our voices are a gift for his glory. Not long ago on my social media, a man said, "A woman in a pulpit with the name of Jesus in her mouth is a witch." When did gender become more powerful than the name of Jesus? For his statement to be true, a woman's voice and a wooden box would undermine the very name of Jesus.

That anyone even thinks this could be a possibility is not only shocking, it is ignorant. And when did the use of a pulpit come into play? Certainly not in the early church where people ministered from house to house and in hidden places. It is the Word of God rather than the word of any person or the elevation of any pulpit that carries authority. The gender of the person speaking the name of Jesus cannot increase or diminish its power.

Our voices are a gift for his glory.

In the early church, there were no pulpits or even Bibles for that matter. More often than not, they met in secret and in homes. Often these "worship services" weren't on Sundays, and they looked nothing like ours today. Some met on the Sabbath; others met every day and from house to house. Let's be careful we are not enshrining our cultural bias by superimposing it on theirs. The very ones who warn us against reading Scripture in light of their cultural context are often guilty of imposing our cultural context on the first century Christians. There were no pulpits for men let alone women to stand behind in their day. In our day, podcasts, social media, books, audiobooks, television, and even YouTube have all become platforms that people speak on and are in many ways pulpits of sorts. Does a church building make a sermon holy, or is it the testimony of Jesus and the Word of God that do that?

Having said all this, beloved goddaughter, be free to follow wherever you feel your Lord is leading you. If you feel led to be silent, be silent. If you feel led to preach, then preach unafraid. Obey your King, but I beg you, do not allow the traditions of religion to make the power of the gospel void in your life. Don't listen to those who say that women in the church are a problem, for, surely, they are an answer.

Jesus died to fully redeem both male and female. We have not been redeemed in the likeness of Eve to be returned to a garden. We have been redeemed in the likeness of our Prince and welcomed into a glorious kingdom where none can be silent about the wonder and grace of the Most High God, their heavenly Father.

Godmother Conversation Starters

Has the gift of God on your life been shut down or celebrated?

Do you believe God is the one who gave you a voice?

Start a discussion about head coverings. Is Jesus our covering or is it a piece of cloth?

What are some ways you can celebrate the gift of God on another woman's life?

Eleven

When Godmothers and Goddaughters Connect

For whoever does the will of my Father in heaven is my brother and sister and mother.

—Matthew 12:50

I remember the moment I met Hosanna. She approached me at a church where we were both ministering. I felt immediately drawn to her. I sensed there was something beautifully unique, sweet, and strong on her life that I needed to bless. As we worshiped alongside one another that night, I tucked her away in my heart with the whisper, *goddaughter*. Later I watched in awe as she ministered a spoken word with such tender authority. After service, we exchanged numbers and almost as quickly as we met, she was off to minister at another church. That was in late autumn. Over the next few months, I lifted her up in prayer whenever she danced across my mind, and we occasionally texted.

Our heavenly Father makes these types of connections for a reason. Three months later, I had a bit more insight on why. Hosanna was about to head into a season of hardship when she was the victim of a trifecta of theft, treachery, and tragedy. The enemy was preparing to open a gap before her in the hope it would swallow her up. Early the next year, John and I traveled first to Vietnam, then to Indonesia. We both contracted a tropical fever while in Vietnam. The illness extended our stay in Indonesia longer than expected because the fever prevented us from traveling. Thankfully, we were with gracious friends. As I tossed and turned in my hotel bed, I found myself praying for Hosanna. Actually, it felt like a battle. I called her as soon as I was back stateside. She is a very private person, so I had no idea what she had been through, and it wasn't until much later that she shared her story with me.

In that short span of time, she had been lied about, stolen from, and physically assaulted by a pastor. The following is a portion of her story:

> I felt like I had lost everything my ministry was built on. There I was. Taken advantage of. Lied about. And everything I thought my ministry was built on, taken away.
>
> I had already told my husband I was done. My heart was shattered in ways I didn't know was possible.
>
> While sitting on my couch watching television as I had done for a straight week at that point, feeling sorry for myself, broken, and defeated, I saw *Without Rival* on my bookshelf and remembered a fire I once walked by. A fire I once encountered. You had given me the book, and I had started it, but since being overcome with self-pity, had put it down. I paused my TV show. I reopened the book. With every line I read, I was putting up wall after wall after wall. Then my phone rang.

Incoming call: Lisa Bevere.

I've never told anyone that I was reading *Without Rival* at the time. It seemed unreal. Until now, only my husband knew that truth. It was almost too crazy for me to believe myself!

You said, "I have no idea what is happening in your soul, Hosanna. But I am calling to tell you, you can't just sit on your couch and wait passively for God to heal you. Everyone is discouraged right now. There is a real battle going on. You have to fight."

You were right. I was not fighting at all. I was upset at the state of my soul, and I was upset at God for allowing such heartbreak to happen to me.

You said, "This is an attack from the enemy. You'll have to fight back. Discouragement has been creeping into our leaders and churches like spiders. I'm seeing it everywhere. Yes, it's happening to everyone. Make no mistake, lovely one, this will be a fight."

In the chapter I had been reading (that I was trying so hard to ignore), you wrote, "Trials have the power to transform us from who we are into who we long to be. But along the way we picked up the lie that we could be heroes without ever engaging in a battle."[1]

That was me. Refusing to engage in battle. And here you were, personally calling to let me know I will not be a hero without getting off my couch and fighting for my life.

Then you said, "You are loved. Be courageous and true to what is in and on you."

As we hung up the phone, it was like a blindfold fell off my eyes. From that moment on, a fire ignited inside of me. I chose to declare war.

I got off my couch, and the months following involved a lot of hard work, a lot of heart work, a lot of being in the Word, a lot of listening to the voice of the Spirit, a lot of opening up to leaders and pastors I was once afraid to be weak in front of, a lot of writing, a lot of warring in prayer, a lot of trimming the branches of toxic relationships, and a lot of telling the truth to you as you checked in on me and watched as I fanned into flame the determination you had ignited inside of me.

It was one of the hardest seasons of my life. But I had to find my identity in Christ. Not in my reputation. Not in my relationships.

These trials had the power to transform me into who I longed to be—when I fought for it.

You gave me permission.

I learned that we, as the younger generation, need to not assume that those wiser than us don't want to know us, speak to us, or speak truth to us. I learned that some of them don't want us to stand out of the way; they want us to step up. I learned that we need to be bold. I learned that we need to stop making excuses for ourselves. I learned that we need to have the courage to be vulnerable. Because on the other side of our fears and entitlement are men and women with wisdom beyond our years, who have been hearing from the Holy Spirit for years, and God wants to use them to instill inside of us the fire that God has put in them. They've lived through the wars we're currently battling. They've conquered the mountains we're currently facing.

I love you, Lisa. I'll speak truth to the next generation, empowering them in Jesus's name, like you have so graciously spoken to me. I won't compare. I won't compete. All you have shown me, I will pay it forward.

And she is. She is the beautiful and brave Hosanna Poetry (Wong), and I love her. The enemy was trying to break her and get her to quit when actually she was on the verge of a breakthrough. She had hidden herself in a listless posture of distraction, watching show after show to numb the pain of crushed hopes. As she read *Without Rival*, she erected wall after wall to protect herself against yet another round of disappointment. When I called, the lie was exposed for what it was, and the gap was filled. She opened her heart, moved away from despondency, and dared to respond to hope.

> *Quitting is not an option for goddaughters who desire to honor the love of their Father and the sacrifice of his Son.*

Just as I called her, I believe God is calling you to shake yourself and get off whatever couch the enemy has you languishing on. Binge-watching shows is an escape, but it will not win any battle or serve to restore any semblance of vision. Quitting is not an option for goddaughters who desire to honor the love of their Father and the sacrifice of his Son. Yes, your life may look different than you thought it would in this season, but that doesn't mean it is any less sacred. Weep if you must, then rise and lift your voice in song.

A TALE OF THREE WIDOWS

Scripture gives us examples of what happens when the lives of godmothers and goddaughters intersect. The first one I want to explore is the beautiful story of Ruth and Naomi.

I love that there is actually a book in the Bible named after a Moabitess. In many ways, it is rather shocking. This is an account of two women who experience tragedy and great loss only to see it transformed into triumph and restoration.

To move quickly to the latter part of this story, I will summarize how it began. Famine hit the land of Judah, and a family of four sojourned in Moab. Shortly after their arrival, the father died. His widow was named Naomi. Later their two sons married two daughters of the land of Moab. A decade passed, and the two sons followed their father in death. Desolate and childless, Naomi heard that "the LORD had visited his people and given them food" (Ruth 1:6), and she decided to return to Judah. Her two widowed daughters-in-law accompanied her part of the way.

> But Naomi said to her two daughters-in-law, "Go, return each of you to her mother's house. May the LORD deal kindly with you, as you have dealt with the dead and with me. The LORD grant that you may find rest, each of you in the house of her husband!" Then she kissed them, and they lifted up their voices and wept. (Ruth 1:8–9)

Life will always allow us the opportunity to go back. In this situation, returning made more sense than going forward with their mother-in-law. Naomi was too old and had nothing left to offer them. She argued,

> "No, my daughters, for it is exceedingly bitter to me for your sake that the hand of the LORD has gone out against me." Then they lifted up their voices and wept again. And Orpah kissed her mother-in-law, but Ruth clung to her. (Ruth 1:13–14)

Two young widows wept on a road. One went back to the familiar; the other forward to the unknown. Ruth had chosen her course, and she would not be dissuaded.

> But Ruth said, "Do not urge me to leave you or to return from following you. For where you go I will go, and where you lodge I will lodge. Your people shall be my people, and your God my

God. Where you die I will die, and there will I be buried. May the LORD do so to me and more also if anything but death parts me from you." (Ruth 1:16–17)

This is the language of covenant. Ruth committed her life to Naomi and called upon the Lord to act as a witness against her if she broke it. Two widows—one a godmother, the other a goddaughter—walked together to Bethlehem. When they arrived, they were surrounded by the women of the village, who asked, could this be our long-lost friend Naomi?

She said to them, "Do not call me Naomi; call me Mara, for the Almighty has dealt very bitterly with me. I went away full, and the LORD has brought me back empty. Why call me Naomi, when the LORD has testified against me and the Almighty has brought calamity upon me?" (Ruth 1:20–21)

Her name felt like a mockery. *Naomi* means pleasant, delightful, and beautiful. In contrast, *Mara* means bitter, which best described her circumstances. How could Naomi possibly have known she was about to experience a turnabout? These destitute widows arrived at harvest time, so Ruth is sent to glean in the field of one of Naomi's late husband's relatives. Ruth is hard at work in the field when she is noticed.

Then Boaz said to Ruth, "Now, listen, my daughter, do not go to glean in another field or leave this one, but keep close to my young women. Let your eyes be on the field that they are reaping, and go after them. Have I not charged the young men not to touch you? And when you are thirsty, go to the vessels and drink what the young men have drawn." (Ruth 2:8–9)

Overwhelmed by his generosity, Ruth asks him why.

> Then she fell on her face, bowing to the ground, and said to him, "Why have I found favor in your eyes, that you should take notice of me, since I am a foreigner?" But Boaz answered her, "All that you have done for your mother-in-law since the death of your husband has been fully told to me, and how you left your father and mother and your native land and came to a people that you did not know before. (Ruth 2:10–11)

God has ways of making our story known without our help. Boaz was well acquainted with God's grace to foreign outlier women. His mother was Rahab, the harlot of Jericho, and his father was Salmon, one of the spies she hid. Boaz recognized a woman of faith when he saw one. Ruth's devotion to Naomi made her known long before she was seen. And then Boaz prophesied to Ruth.

> The LORD repay you for what you have done, and a full reward be given you by the LORD, the God of Israel, under whose wings you have come to take refuge! (Ruth 2:12)

As I read this verse, I was moved by its beauty. I believe this promise is for every daughter who takes refuge in God. We are all refugees looking for the shelter of the Most High God. Ruth had chosen a future of faith when she refused to turn back. Not many people would follow a destitute widow back to a land where the people were sworn to be her enemies. Somehow Ruth knew that by following Naomi, she was following the God of Naomi.

God has ways of making our story known without our help.

Then she said, "I have found favor in your eyes, my lord, for you have comforted me and spoken kindly to your servant, though I am not one of your servants." (Ruth 2:13)

Ruth was an outlier to the things of God. Boaz, Ruth, and Rahab foreshadow God's coming grace to the gentiles.

Naomi devised a way for Ruth to become Boaz's wife and Boaz their kinsman redeemer. The plan involved Ruth slipping into an all-male gathering at the threshing floor. Once the men were asleep, she uncovered Boaz's feet and lay there. He woke up startled and wondered who was under the covers with him.

He said, "Who are you?" And she answered, "I am Ruth, your servant. Spread your wings over your servant, for you are a redeemer." (Ruth 3:9)

"I am Ruth." This name means companion, friend, and vision of beauty. Then Ruth echoed back to Boaz the word picture he had given her: "Spread your wings over your servant, for you are a redeemer." In that moment, he was no longer only Naomi's kinsman; he became Ruth's redeemer. Boaz promised to redeem her as long as a closer kinsman chose not to.

So she lay at his feet until the morning, but arose before one could recognize another. And he said, "Let it not be known that the woman came to the threshing floor." (Ruth 3:14)

I find this rather funny; obviously someone couldn't keep the whole woman-at-the-threshing-floor thing a secret and wrote it down! Apparently God doesn't have a problem with women slipping into places they're normally not welcomed when it comes to matters of faith and redemption. Both Rahab and

Ruth had discovered the power of exchange. Rahab exchanged the fear of judgment for the fear of the Lord, and Ruth exchanged her people for a place among God's people. The very next day, Boaz sorted out the matter, redeemed Naomi's husband's land, and in the process took Ruth as his wife.

> So Boaz took Ruth, and she became his wife. And he went in to her, and the LORD gave her conception, and she bore a son. (Ruth 4:13)

The phrase *the LORD gave her conception* made me wonder if up to this point Ruth was barren. She was married for ten years before she was widowed, and suddenly there's a son. God was not just in the process of restoring Ruth's life; there was restoration for Naomi as well.

> Then the women said to Naomi, "Blessed be the LORD, who has not left you this day without a redeemer, and may his name be renowned in Israel! He shall be to you a restorer of life and a nourisher of your old age, for your daughter-in-law who loves you, who is more to you than seven sons, has given birth to him." (Ruth 4:14–15)

The same women Naomi told to call her Mara (bitter) are calling her blessed. How amazing. Naomi only hoped to bless Ruth, but the blessing came back full circle to her as well. God always had a plan. Naomi's life was no longer bitter and empty because her heart and arms were full. The women surrounding Naomi prophesied the promise of legacy.

> Then Naomi took the child and laid him on her lap and became his nurse. And the women of the neighborhood gave him a

name, saying, "A son has been born to Naomi." They named him Obed. He was the father of Jesse, the father of David. (Ruth 4:16–17)

These two women foreshadow the story of God's grace. Naomi is a daughter of the law who saw herself under God's judgment only to experience abundant grace because Ruth understood that God's love superseded the law. In his book *The Romance of Redemption*, M. R. De Haan explores this concept in detail.

> Ruth was a Gentile and thus barred from the covenant nation by the law. She was legally excluded. But in addition, she was a Moabite concerning whom the law says in Deuteronomy 23:3, "An Ammonite or Moabite shall not enter into the congregation of the LORD . . ."
>
> The law shut Ruth out, but grace took her in. By her marriage to Boaz, the Hebrew kinsman-redeemer, she entered the favored family of Israel. All this is a picture of the grace of God in Jesus Christ, our Kinsman Boaz, who took us, who were condemned under the law, aliens and strangers to God, doomed to death and destruction, and made us, by His redeeming work, the sons of God and members of the first family of heaven.[2]

My hope is that every discouraged godmother will look beyond her own grief, loss, and disappointment and discover that she yet has the power to bless the goddaughters that surround her. Naomi sent Ruth to the threshing field with this hope.

> Then Naomi her mother-in-law said to her, "My daughter, should I not seek rest for you, that it may be well with you?" (Ruth 3:1)

In seeking rest and provision for her God-given daughter, Naomi experienced it herself. In positioning Ruth to be Boaz's wife, Naomi recovered her lost legacy. In being faithful to a God that she imagined angry and possibly faithless to her, she modeled something for us all to follow. Trials are trails and pathways of preparation rather than the end of the story. Your life will end with God's faithfulness. If the ending isn't evident here, it will be revealed in eternity. God is faithful and his plan is redemptive.

Trials are trails and pathways of preparation rather than the end of the story.

By being faithful to her God-given mother, Ruth found herself in the lineage of Christ. None of us can tell where our choices might lead, but I can assure you that they live on long after we've left this earth. What began with three widows weeping on the road to Bethlehem was part of the story of the King of Kings.

THE IMPOSSIBLE MEETS THE IMPROBABLE

The New Testament gives us another example, through the lives of Mary and Elizabeth, of what happens when godmothers and goddaughters connect. Both of these women model a pattern for us to contemplate and follow today. Because of this, I want to examine their lives of obedience and sanctification believing they hold present promise.

Mary and Elizabeth lived in a time when women had little to no voice, yet their private conversation was captured in the canons of Scripture for us to hear.

To set the scene in the book of Luke, there's an awful king in power and a godly, priestly, old couple who are barren. We immediately see the potential for quite a few challenges. This couple, Zechariah and Elizabeth, served God under corrupt leadership. Herod was the king who would later order all boys under the age of two killed when he learned of the birth of Jesus. This couple lived exemplary lives, yet Elizabeth was barren. Just like their ancestors of faith, Abraham and Sarah, without divine intervention, any hope of a child was gone.

Everything changed in one day. Zechariah was serving in the temple when the honor of serving in the Holy Place fell to him. One priest went in while the other priests remained outside with the worshipers. The altar of incense was right outside the Holy of Holies, and it represented the fragrance of prayer.

> All at once an angel of the Lord appeared to him, standing just to the right of the altar of incense.
>
> Zechariah was startled and overwhelmed with fear. But the angel reassured him, saying, "Don't be afraid, Zechariah! God is showing grace to you. For I have come to tell you that *your prayer for a child has been answered*. Your wife, Elizabeth, will bear you a son and you are to name him John." (Luke 1:11–13 TPT)

But, when the angel finished, Zechariah had some questions. You'd think Zechariah would have started doing a happy dance, but he didn't.

> Zechariah asked the angel, "How do you expect me to believe this? I'm an old man and my wife is too old to give me a child. What sign can you give me to prove this will happen?" (Luke 1:18 TPT)

The sign was silence. Zechariah would not speak again until the child was born.

Soon afterward his wife, Elizabeth, became pregnant and went into seclusion for the next five months. She said with joy, "See how kind it is of God to gaze upon me and take away the disgrace of my barrenness!" (Luke 1:24–25 TPT)

I love this woman! She is pregnant and goes into seclusion. If it had been me, my old pregnant body would be on display at the well for all to see (especially with Zechariah not talking). But Elizabeth understood that what she carried within her was more important than proving herself in public. It was enough to have her private, very intimate disgrace removed. She reveled in the kindness and goodness of God to her.

The scene shifts from an aged godmother to a young virgin goddaughter.

During the sixth month of Elizabeth's pregnancy, the angel Gabriel was sent from God's presence to an unmarried girl named Mary, living in Nazareth, a village in Galilee. She was engaged to a man named Joseph, a true descendant of King David. (Luke 1:26–27 TPT)

Gabriel is visiting earth again with another message. This time it is for a young woman.

Gabriel appeared to her and said, "Grace to you, young woman, for the Lord is with you and so you are anointed with great favor."

Mary was deeply troubled over the words of the angel and bewildered over what this may mean for her. But the angel reassured her, saying, "Do not yield to your fear, Mary, for the Lord has found delight in you and has chosen to surprise you with a wonderful gift." (Luke 1:28–30 TPT)

Surprises are good, but this one was totally unexpected.

> You will become pregnant with a baby boy, and you are to name him Jesus. He will be supreme and will be known as the Son of the Highest. And the Lord God will enthrone him as King on his ancestor David's throne. He will reign as King of Israel forever, and his reign will have no limit. (Luke 1:31–33 TPT)

Then Mary raised a reasonable question:

> Mary said, "But how could this happen? I am still a virgin!" (Luke 1:34 TPT)

Her question of *How could this happen?* was very different than Zechariah's question, *How do you expect me to believe you?* He questioned the integrity of the messenger; the other questioned the method.

> Gabriel answered, "The Spirit of Holiness will fall upon you and almighty God will spread his shadow of power over you in a cloud of glory! This is why the child born to you will be holy, and he will be called the Son of God." (Luke 1:35 TPT)

Then the angel let Mary in on a secret:

> What's more, your aged aunt, Elizabeth, has also become pregnant with a son. The "barren one" is now in her sixth month. (Luke 1:36 TPT)

The impossible was confirmed by the improbable. How beautiful that Elizabeth, who'd been known as the *barren one,* became the blessed one with life blooming within her. Then hear the next verse, lovely goddaughter, because it is a promise made to all of us:

> Not one promise from God is empty of power, for with God there is no such thing as impossibility! (Luke 1:37 TPT)

Not one.

The ESV simply says it this way: "For nothing will be impossible with God" (Luke 1:37).

There is power attached to every promise of God because the Promiser is all powerful. Many things are impossible *without God*, but *with God*, nothing is. In the words of Gabriel, I heard the resound of Abraham, our father of faith:

> No unbelief made him waver concerning the promise of God, but he grew strong in his faith as he gave glory to God, fully convinced that *God was able to do what he had promised*. (Rom. 4:20–21)

Mary was chosen, but a virgin birth was an impossibility without God.

> And Mary said, "Behold, I am the servant of the Lord; let it be to me according to your word." And the angel departed from her. (Luke 1:38)

What might happen if a generation of God's daughters echoed this refrain? Father, we are your servants, let your Word have its way in our lives. Sweet one, you don't have to work it up or figure it out. Simply declare yourself willing to live according to his Word.

> *Even now, I believe a generation of improbable women are rising to bless daughters who carry what seem to be impossible promises.*

I love what happens next. Mary, the daughter who carries within her the promised Messiah, goes to Elizabeth, the consecrated one, who carries within her the prophet.

> Afterward, Mary arose and hurried off to the hill country of Judea, to the village where Zechariah and Elizabeth lived. (Luke 1:39 TPT)

Mary hastened to be with her cousin Elizabeth. She knew that what she carried within her was more than she could carry forward on her own. Mary needed another woman who would understand what she had been entrusted with. Even now, I believe a generation of improbable women are rising to bless daughters who carry what seem to be impossible promises. I believe it is the very reason the enemy has worked so hard to separate the mothers and the daughters.

> Arriving at their home, Mary entered the house and greeted Elizabeth. At the moment she heard Mary's voice, the baby within Elizabeth's womb jumped and kicked. And suddenly, Elizabeth was filled to overflowing with the Holy Spirit! (Luke 1:40–41 TPT)

The life within Elizabeth responded to the sound of Mary's voice. Something leaps within us when godmothers and goddaughters connect. In this moment, when two women met, John, Elizabeth's son, was filled with the Holy Spirt as promised by Gabriel. This infilling spilled over to the one who carried him as well, and Elizabeth could not help but prophesy this glorious mystery:

With a loud voice she prophesied with power:

> "Mary! You are a woman given the highest favor
>   and privilege above all others.
>   For your child is destined to bring God great delight.
> How did I deserve such a remarkable honor
>   to have the mother of my Lord come and visit me?
> The moment you came in the door and greeted me,
>   my baby danced inside me with ecstatic joy!
> Great favor is upon you, *for you have believed*
>   *every word spoken to you from the Lord*." (Luke
>   1:42–45 TPT)

It is important to note that Elizabeth could not have possibly known the words that had passed between Gabriel and Mary. And what could have made Elizabeth imagine that Mary, a virgin, was with child? Nothing. The Holy Spirit knew. Those who are filled with the Spirit know things by the Spirit. You also know others by the Spirit.

Elizabeth rejoiced because Mary believed.

Elizabeth carried within her John (God's gracious gift), who celebrated what Mary carried within her, Jesus (Emmanuel, God with us). Let's be women who recognize and honor what one another carry. This recognition flows both ways: godmothers celebrating their goddaughters and goddaughters celebrating their godmothers.

This is how God planned for us to live: as women who are thrilled that each of us simply dared to believe. We will see this happen when women choose to celebrate rather than compete with one another. Far too often, the snare of competition hinders this relational blessing.

If you can't find these types of women, it simply means you get to be that woman for others. Don't be afraid; it always has to start with someone. Why shouldn't it be you?

Mary knew she'd need the wisdom of a woman who had known some tough stuff. Being known as the barren one would have been rough for Elizabeth. When you are looking for a godmother, watch for women who have been through some rough stuff and have come out stronger on the other side. I find it interesting that Mary didn't run to her mother but to a godmother, and the two of them spent three months together. I wish I could've listened in on the conversations of these women, pregnant with impossible promise.

The reproach of Eve was stripped away as the forerunner and the Redeemer were entrusted to two women.

Their lives are a refrain of our Father's faithfulness. The reproach of Eve was stripped away as the forerunner and the Redeemer were entrusted to two women. It is my prayer that as we see one another, we will know and bless each other as living testaments of God's faithfulness. What a confirmation Elizabeth's words must have been for Mary. As an unwed virgin, she was about to face some unknowns. But for the moment, her soul overflowed!

And Mary said,

> "My soul magnifies the Lord,
>   and my spirit rejoices in God my Savior,
> for he has looked on the humble estate of his servant.
>   For behold, from now on all generations will call me
>   blessed;

for he who is mighty has done great things for me,
and holy is his name.
And his mercy is for those who fear him
from generation to generation.
He has shown strength with his arm;
he has scattered the proud in the thoughts of
their hearts;
he has brought down the mighty from their thrones
and exalted those of humble estate;
he has filled the hungry with good things,
and the rich he has sent away empty.
He has helped his servant Israel,
in remembrance of his mercy,
as he spoke to our fathers,
to Abraham and to his offspring forever."
(Luke 1:46–55)

These beautiful prophetic words were recorded for all human-kind to hear. Perhaps it was the silent Zechariah who wrote them down as he wiped away tears of wonder. Regardless of how this interchange was captured, may we, the daughters of our day, hear and know so that we might echo them in our own way, in our own time, in word and deed. By so intimately involving women in his redemptive plan, God was restoring the precedent that had begun in the garden . . . women are answers, not problems.

What is that improbable promise of God in your life?

Maybe we are not hearing because we have been deaf to the voices of one another for too long. Godmothers, imagining that the goddaughters don't need them, have lapsed into silence. Goddaughters have imagined that the mothers won't be there for them, but both are blinded by a lie that wants to isolate us from the legacy we carry.

Maybe you identify with one of these women. Perhaps you feel like:

Naomi, the one who suffered unspeakable loss. If so, take heart; God is not angry at you. Don't you dare change your name to bitterness. Even though you imagine you've lost everything, there is more within you than you know. Pour blessing out of your brokenness. Smile, because your story isn't over. There is a daughter who loves you waiting for your words of instruction. Don't push her aside or turn her away. Help her, and you will find laughter, legacy, and life on the other side.

Ruth, an outlier daughter of noble character who is new to the things of God. Don't be dissuaded by the older women who may try to turn you away saying that they have nothing for you. Draw it out of them. You are part of a new family of faith. Leave your land of loss, and go into new fields of harvest and glean all that was left behind for you. Labor as a woman of honor who shares her provision with others. Get ready to be surprised with God's legacy and life.

Elizabeth, the consecrated one with a long legacy of godliness. Come out of hiding. We know your secret; there is life within you. Do you see the daughters gathered at your door? Listen for the sound of their voices, their greeting will quicken the Spirit of God within you. Bless those who dare to believe. Sing with them. Pour into them, holy woman of God. Let what is in you be related to what is in them.

Mary, highly favored of God. Be astounded, brave one, but don't walk alone. You are chosen; let God's living Word accomplish the impossible in and through you. Magnify God in humility and wonder. Embrace holiness. Find that godmother who understands what you carry and who will help you know how to steward the gift on your life in beauty and strength.

You see, I actually believe we are beginning to hear one another's voices.

I believe there's a fresh outpouring of God's Spirit that will empower the godmothers to bless rather than curse what God is doing among the young women and men. There is a grace on the older women to celebrate the hand of promise on the younger generation rather than rehearse their own disappointments. No matter what, we cannot allow another generation of women to be shut down. Nor can we let them imagine that serving Christ is the equivalent of becoming a pseudocelebrity. It is a call that is sacred. Even if we don't understand *how* they are doing things, we should be able to bless the *why*.

Go ahead and reach out. You are not alone, lovely; don't be afraid to approach a woman who has gone before you. Even if the first woman you reach out for doesn't reach back, don't stop. Someone will respond. And while you wait, reach back to younger women.

I never dreamed that Hosanna would ever have gone through so much. I still remember talking to her. In all honesty, at the time I wasn't even sure she heard me. I just knew I couldn't be silent when I felt something so beautiful and strong stirring within her.

Time has taught me that God longs to transform our setbacks into setups.

But it won't fall out of the sky; you have to get up and let him.

So, lovely goddaughter, I need to know.

Have you withdrawn from the field that you meant to glean in?

What couch are you sitting on? Perhaps you're not binge-watching; maybe you're scrolling, shopping, binge-eating, arguing online, hiding in your work or behind

God longs to transform our setbacks into setups.

217

your children. Whether your shield is a front of being busy, living vicariously, or pretending that one more possession will make you happy, I'm here to tell you it won't. You were made for more. Entertainment and stuff will leave you empty, and being busy will leave you exhausted.

It's time to embrace the risk of living your life. Yes, daughter, heal for a season if you've been wounded. Fight to forgive if you've been wronged. Rest, by all means, to recover your strength. A temporary retreat to assess your position is okay. But withdrawing is not an option.

Godmother Conversation Starters

Is there what seems to be an impossible promise stirring inside you?

If you're young, think of an older woman you can connect with.

If you're older, think of a younger woman to reach out to.

Twelve

When Godmothers and Goddaughters Collide

The goal of confrontation is restoration rather than alienation.

—Lisa Bevere

It was time. Actually, it was far past time. There was unresolved conflict in the air, and I had no idea why.

Over the years, I'd reached out only to receive one-word responses. She was not going to engage with me. In an attempt to figure it out, I'd asked all the questions I knew to ask. I'd spoken with all the people I knew to speak with. Which was odd because most of the time when I've done something wrong, I know what I've done. Often, right away.

If there was to be any resolution, I'd have to take a more direct approach. And if I was unable to resolve this, then what had already happened once was going to happen again.

I was slightly confused and definitely nervous. But more than both of these, I wanted it right. I don't like unfinished business and chapters without endings. Nor do I like to navigate disagreements when I have no idea what the disagreement is about. I didn't know *what* the problem was, but Jesus was very clear about *how* it was to be handled. In Matthew 5:23–24, Jesus says,

> So if you are offering your gift at the altar and there remember that your brother [or sister] has something against you, leave your gift there before the altar and go. First be reconciled to your brother [or sister], and then come and offer your gift.

I found myself wondering if all of this really applied. After all, I was at home. I wasn't in a temple presenting an offering. Wasn't it her problem? Hadn't I texted . . . twice? I'd opened the door, but it wasn't reciprocated. She obviously had something against me, a grudge or some other form of a serious misunderstanding that she had no interest in resolving. Which raised another question: Was she even a friend? I'd been there for her, but it was a one-way street, and now she wanted nothing more to do with me. At least this was the construct of reasoning I had housed in my mind.

I knew from experience the very fact I was being so stubborn and looking for ways to excuse myself from addressing this meant it was important that I did. Even if only for my sake. I didn't have an altar or an offering, but as you read the words of Jesus it is hard to miss the sense of urgency. I don't know if it is the same for you, but when I am in prayer, that's exactly the time when I remember relational breaches. I used to see these as interruptions rather than the prompting of the Holy Spirit. Now I know they are invitations to make things right.

In the past, I would push the thoughts aside and continue to pray or read my Bible or devotional. Sometimes I was proactive and posted a Scripture, recorded a thought, worshiped a little louder, or made some message notes. When these thoughts came unbidden, I thought they were distractions and ignored them. Sadly, by doing so, I chose the lesser thing.

The Message paraphrase of Matthew 5:23 reads this way:

This is *how* I want you to conduct yourself in these matters. If you enter your place of worship and, about to make an offering, you suddenly remember a grudge a friend has against you . . .

Most of us don't have traditional altars in our places of worship. What happens at the altar is far more important than what constitutes an altar. Altars are places of consecration, and our obedience is our offering. Ultimately, any true offering is an act of obedient surrender, prayer, service, and exchange. Offerings can take on many forms. Offerings are simply anything that God has gifted and empowered you to offer. Anything that is given in his name is considered holy. An offering can be a petition, prayer, time, or a talent.

As we prepare to give what we have been given to the high and holy One, he's even more concerned about what we've left behind. It might look like this.

You're just about to pray over a meal, and suddenly you remember . . . you spoke harshly to your children. You're serving in any capacity at a church or conference, and suddenly you remember . . . you were hateful to your husband. You are about to give what is in your power, and suddenly you remember . . . there is a breach in a friendship. Maybe you're about to sing on stage or speak from a platform, and suddenly you remember. You're in a time of prayer, and suddenly you remember. I think you've got the point.

As the offering comes in contact with the altar, you *suddenly remember* someone is less than happy with you.

That someone could be anyone. Maybe that someone is your husband, a friend, a coworker, or even one of your children. But more important—who is reminding you?

Whenever any of us are in a holy place or are paused in a holy posture preparing to offer something to our Holy Father, more than likely it is the Holy Spirit who is *suddenly reminding* us.

I have no problem remembering who has upset me . . . even when I'm busy. I hear it even in the noise. I rarely miss harsh words, petty remarks, fragments of gossip, full-on slander, and verbal assaults. These types of infractions put a demand on my attention.

But in the stillness, it's a different story altogether.

When my soul is quiet, I sense the pain and disappointment that *I* have caused others. In the solitude, I suddenly remember those I've upset. I hear their tone or remember mine. When my eyes are closed, I see the look that I failed to catch in the light. I perceive nuances I missed in the moment.

In the solitude, I suddenly remember those I've upset.

When I'm alone, I often realize I've lost touch with someone.

As we draw near to God, we'll discover our distance with others. When a breach is remembered, it's time to respond.

Often the quickest way to the heart of our Father is by loving his children.

Intimacy is no easy achievement. . . . But if the costs are considerable, the rewards are magnificent, for in relationship with another and with the God who loves us we complete the humanity for which we were created.

Eugene Peterson[1]

We draw near to God as we close the gaps between those he loves.

The next verse in the Message paraphrase reads,

Abandon your offering, *leave immediately,* go to this friend and *make things right.* Then and only then, come back and work things out with God. (Matt. 5:24)

Abandon is a strong word!

It means to walk out on, cancel, and vacate the premises. The ESV admonishes us, "Leave your gift there before the altar" (Matt. 5:24). This is vivid imagery . . . I can almost hear Jesus say, "back away from the offering, drop the microphone, put away the gift, lay down your phone, put down your Bible study, set aside the devotional, stop singing, and run, do not walk. It's not offering time; it is time to make things right!"

That day in prayer, I pushed aside all the reasoning and excuses and acknowledged what needed to happen. I told my husband what I was going to do (for accountability), and I took steps to get in touch with her. I've learned that if I don't do things right away, they can get away from me.

We were ministering together at the same event soon, and things would just be too uncomfortable for both of us if this breach was not addressed and resolved.

I'm ashamed to admit, I'd wrestled with this disconnect for three years and was none the wiser. I wasn't even sure if I had her correct number. I sent a text message and asked for a conversation, then put my phone down and walked out of the room.

She replied she would be able to talk the following day.

Now the question arose: What would I say?

Three years is a long time to leave something unresolved and flapping in the wind.

WHAT RECONCILIATION MEANS TO GOD

Jesus's words in Matthew confirm the incredible importance he places on relationships. People will always mean more to Jesus than an offering. There is a divine connection between what we offer and our heart. How can we ever give our best to God when we've been at our worst with others? In the book of Malachi in the Old Testament, we see similar problems—and we still face them today.

> *How can we ever give our best to God when we've been at our worst with others?*

Malachi was addressing a corrupt priesthood, widespread divorce, injustice, a lifeless routine of worship, the neglect of tithing, and subpar offerings. First, the prophet asks why anyone would give God what they would not dare to offer their governor. Then he goes on to explain why their prayers and offerings aren't met with their expected outcome.

> You cover the LORD's altar with tears, with weeping and groaning because he no longer regards the offering or accepts it with favor from your hand. (Mal. 2:13)

And what would possibly cause God to disconnect from their offerings this time? They were breaking covenant with their wives. This gives us some insight into how much God honors the marriage union. He unites us with a portion of the Spirit.

> But you say, "Why does he not?" Because the LORD was witness between you and the wife of your youth, to whom you have been faithless, though she is your companion and your wife by covenant. Did he not make them one, with a portion of the Spirit in their union? (Mal. 2:14–15)

The Message paraphrase of Malachi 2:13–14 reads:

> And here's a second offense: You fill the place of worship with your whining and sniveling because you don't get what you want from GOD. Do you know why? Simple. Because GOD was there as a witness when you spoke your marriage vows to your young bride, and now you've broken those vows, broken the faith-bond with your vowed companion, your covenant wife.

Altars are where we learn what God wants rather than places we go to get what we want.

Altars are where we meet with our Father so he can tell us who we need to meet with.

Altars are where we bring our all. God is more concerned with what is in our hearts than with what is in our hands. It isn't about how much time, talent, or resource we give. It's about the heart of the giver.

He invites us to worship him by first loving others.

As Paul closes his letter in 2 Corinthians 13:11, he sums up the value God places on how we treat one another:

Finally, brothers, rejoice. Aim for restoration, comfort one another, agree with one another, live in peace; and the God of love
and peace will be with you.

Restoration is our aim, and as we live in peace with one another, God's love and peace overshadow us. I needed to restore
this relationship if at all possible.

When the arranged time of our talk arrived, I stepped outside. I didn't want any interruptions or distractions. I dialed
her number and held my breath.

She answered the phone. It was up to me to take the lead.
I explained that when I had met her, I had loved her. Wanting
absolutely nothing. I reminded her that I was there for her
when she went through a major transition. I went on to say
how excited I had been when I learned that we would be part
of an event together. I had gone to her session to cheer her on,
and she had snubbed me by acknowledging each of the speakers
from the stage but me . . . twice.

At first, I thought she might have been nervous. Anyone who
has ever been on a stage in front of a thousand-plus people
knows it is easy to forget something or someone. But then it
happened again the next morning.

After explaining how it all looked to me, I asked, "Have I
done something to upset you?"

There was an extraordinarily long pause. Then an audible
intake of air.

Then a wail . . .

I thought, *Dear Jesus, what have I done?* Whatever it was,
it must have been awful! Through muffled cries, she explained
it wasn't me. That she was surprised that I of all people would
be the one to call.

She shared that she had been repeatedly wounded by her mother and the women she saw as mother figures in her life. She had pulled away from them all, including me. I was guilty by my association with other women who had injured her.

I listened . . . carefully. I heard what she said as well as what was implied and left unsaid. Her raw vulnerability made a way for both of us to have an honest and open conversation. Not in defense of but to lend insight to what she might have experienced, I shared that many women of her generation have sent mixed messages to the women of mine. They've behaved as though they have life all figured out and don't need our involvement, affirmation, input, or support. It has often felt as though the sacrifices of the women who have walked before them have been marginalized.

We both acknowledged the hurt, the loss, the disconnect. We knew there existed a very real gap and spoke of ways we could bridge it. Of ways we could love and live better as mentors and friends.

It wasn't until later, after I had hung up, that I realized just how wrong I had been. I was the older one, which meant I should have been more mature.

I *never* should have allowed three years to go by without addressing it. For a thousand days, I allowed something to go unsettled and unhealed in *both* of us because of an offense to my pride.

Yes, I had felt disrespected and devalued; who hasn't felt that way? But my reaction was the fruit of wounded pride.

Proverbs 13:10 tells us, "Only by pride cometh contention: but with the well advised is wisdom" (KJV). My wounded pride had left me in the dark. I was blind to it because I hadn't dealt with it.

Whenever we are under the sway of pride, it is as though blinders are put on us, and we see neither what is to the left nor the right. We are trapped in the tunnel vision of self. We cannot see anyone else's pain because we are far too consumed by our own. The crazy thing is, I had seen myself as the victim and the other person as prideful, when actually the roles were reversed.

When I saw her later at the event, my heart welled up with love for her. We embraced. I attended her session, and she was there for mine. There was a moment during worship when I felt compelled to place my hand on her back, but I was concerned it might be a violation of her person and the intimacy of her personal worship. I looked over and noticed that another friend saw my hand hovering behind her, and as if she knew the question lingering in my mind, she nodded her assent . . . do it.

I laid my hand on her back, and the young woman crumbled, then turned and fell into my arms. I don't remember all that I prayed, but as the sound of worship enveloped us both, I remember breaking word curses off of her that had been spoken over her by the women who had passed through her life. Something deep and holy happened. Something that to this day we still don't completely understand but that would not have ever happened if I had remained trapped in pride and offense.

Later she wrote:

> This Sicilian godmother prayed over me for healing as a daughter of God, areas I didn't realize I still needed. Weeks later, God burdened me to stop shrinking back from the role of a spiritual mother. God is raising up spiritual mothers for a generation of girls coming behind us, but we can't step into that role until we are healed in our identity as a daughter. Find the

women ahead of you in life who are interested in legacy, who are holding out a hand and lifting you up. Ones who aren't guarding their influence, but giving it away. They are the front runners, the ones who paved roads of leadership we now walk on freely. Let's take those same kind of risks for the generation coming up next.[2]

Let's be those godmothers and goddaughters. Let's identify with one another and settle our identity in him. We know that we are all goddaughters because we are all God's daughters; let's make the choice to be mothers as well.

HONORABLE IN THE SIGHT OF ALL

We live in a day when it is more common for people to wound one another than to heal, to hate than to love, to argue than to bring peace. We are quicker to alienate and believe the worst about one another than to risk believing the best. Healing takes a lot more work and time than an injury. Loving someone means they can get close enough to hurt you. And arguing to make your point is always easier than working toward peace.

It's time for godmothers and goddaughters to model reconciliation. This means there has never been a riper environment for us to be countercultural to the one we are in. Whenever it is easier to be cruel than it is to be kind, we have that chance to model something very different. For it is in the darkness that light shines brightest. Romans 12:17–18 reads,

> Repay no one evil for evil, but give thought to do what is honorable in the sight of all. If possible, so far as it depends on you, live peaceably with all.

The phrase *honorable in the sight of all* implies that people are observing our lives; the concept of being watched has never been truer. Acting in a manner that is honorable requires a lot of thought and intent. When we are mistreated, we cannot only consider how it feels to us; we must also be aware of how our response to the interaction might look to others. I am not here to argue and correct everybody; I am here to walk in a manner that is in keeping with my profession of Christ.

In many ways, our world has become a very large stage that fits in your hand. How do you want to be seen? What does it look like to be honorable?

The Passion Translation for Romans 12:17–18 reads,

> Never hold a grudge or try to get even, but plan your life around the noblest way to benefit others. Do your best to live as everybody's friend.

This can be as simple as being generous with kindness. We can't be friends *with* everybody, but we can be a friend *to* everyone. Romans 12:19–21 continues,

> Beloved, never avenge yourselves, but leave it to the wrath of God, for it is written, "Vengeance is mine, I will repay, says the Lord." To the contrary, "if your enemy is hungry, feed him; if he is thirsty, give him something to drink; for by so doing you will heap burning coals on his head." Do not be overcome by evil, but overcome evil with good.

Never avenge yourself. Don't do the slap back . . . ever. Leave it to God. Good will win. Justice will be done. Let's keep our hands clean and our hearts pure. God asks us to be kind to our enemies. Nowhere do I read that we are to alienate anyone from the goodness of God. Reconciliation is a pretty big deal to God! Second Corinthians 5:18 reminds us that the ministry of reconciliation comes from Christ: "All this is from God, who through Christ reconciled us to himself and gave us the ministry of reconciliation."

This doesn't mean you have to fix everything for everyone. No single person, not even a spouse, can fill every gap. There are gaps that each of us carry that only God can fill. It is important to ask yourself, *is this a person gap or a God gap?* Is this an opportunity for growth, or are they in need of encouragement or rescue?

> *There are gaps that each of us carry that only God can fill.*

Some people are not safe for you to reconcile with. Perhaps they will be one day, but if they aren't now, then I give you permission to bless them from afar in prayer and to maintain a safe distance. As we work to repair our relationships, it's good to remember the difference. If you're not sure how to determine this, invite someone else into the conversation. Go to people you can really trust. Now let's talk about what those people might look like.

IN YOUR CORNER

You've heard the term *in your corner*. They are the people who act as coaches, trainers, and healers when life threatens to beat us up. Imagine a boxing match, and you're one of the contenders. These friends jump over the ropes or lean in close to whisper when there is a break between rounds. They have an intimate vantage point on what you are going through. As they tend your wounds, they listen to both your fears and protests ("I can't do this . . . it's too hard . . . it's taking too long"), and they answer back, "Yes, you can!" They know when to push you, and they know when to give you permission to rest and return to fight another day.

They know your weaknesses but choose to look you in the eye and remind you of your strengths. They are not merely for you; they are for the bigger thing this battle represents in your life. They remind you that there is hope on the other side of your struggle. These are the friends who champion your growth. These are the relationships that Proverbs describes as,

> Iron sharpens iron,
>> and one man sharpens another. (27:17)

You are in one another's lives to hone each other. Not everyone who crosses your path can or should be this. Another version of Proverbs 27:17 reads: "You use steel to sharpen steel, and one friend sharpens another" (MSG). These types of friendships have to be forged of the same metal. The substance is the same even if the form looks different. You cannot use metals of differing tensile strengths to sharpen one another. If you try to sharpen steel with aluminum, you will end up shredding the aluminum and dulling the steel.

Over the course of a lifetime, you will not have many of these friendships, but treasure the ones you have, don't take them for granted, and invest in them. Hopefully your husband, immediate family, and some of your sacred community will fall under this category. These types of relationships are *transformational*.

IN THE ROOM

Then there is another type of relationship. Let's describe it as the people who are in the room. These types of friendships are seasonal or centered on convenience or commonality. People who are in the room see what is going on, but they are not close enough to hear your whispers. People who are in the room clap when the crowds clap, but they rarely remain when you lose. It doesn't make them bad people. It doesn't mean you aren't worthy of relationship. Don't allow it to wound you. Lovely one, please understand it's not personal. For one reason or another, it is how they've chosen to be related to you.

In the past, this dynamic confused me. Recently, I texted someone who I thought was in my corner. I'd been there for her on a number of occasions when she needed me. When she was in a different season, she couldn't be bothered to text back. Later I was at an event with a mutual friend who I knew she saw as someone that was advantageous to maintain a relationship with. As an experiment, I took a selfie with this friend, sent it her way, and, sure enough, there was an immediate response. Even though the revelation was disappointing, it was actually helpful. I knew what to expect going forward. We are both busy people, and I now knew my relationship with her was purely *transactional*.

Like me, you will be vulnerable to injury when you confuse your transactional relationships (friendships of convenience) with your transformational (intimate connections for growth) ones. Transactional relationships will be in your room as long as it is in their best interest, but when they leave, don't get mad or beg them to come back. Bless them and let them go. And, if they want to come back into your room, let them, but don't attach the wrong expectations to the relationship.

You will always be disappointed when you go to the wrong people looking for the right thing.

You will always be disappointed when you go to the wrong people looking for the right thing. Here are some guidelines for your consideration. True friends are there when you need them, not just when they need something from you. True friends text back when you text them and call back when you call them. It might not be instantaneous or even the same day, but there will be a response. It may be as simple as, "I'll get back with you when I catch my breath." Close friends acknowledge you. If this isn't happening, then you're probably in a transactional relationship.

You will always be disappointed when you go to the wrong people looking for the right thing.

For clarity's sake, I am not talking about people who are busy. We are all far busier than we should be, and there are seasons of hardship, loss, or sickness that naturally slow or stop our ability to respond. I am talking about people who can't be bothered. Having said this, be there for them when they need you. But be careful about attaching any expectations to your actions. Make deposits in their lives, but don't expect a return. Goddaughters, learn from me. I've been wounded when I attached transformational relationship expectations to my transactional friendships.

OUR NEIGHBORS

You shall love the Lord your God with all your heart and with all your soul and with all your strength and with all your mind, and your neighbor as yourself. (Luke 10:27)

We can only love others to the extent that we have learned to become enveloped in God's love. Neighbors are those we see. They are in our neighborhood, where we work, where we grocery shop, on our streets, and where we worship. It is always easier to feel compassion for those we cannot see. Sorry. It is harder to be involved with those we can touch. Sending a check is easier than actually checking on someone who might need more from you than money. It is scary but it needs to happen, because far too many people are far too isolated from one another. I travel and stand on stages in front of a lot of people, so I have to be intentional to connect with people who are in my near. It begins with my family, then my team, and then extends to the women in my area who wish to gather in my home and grow.

> If you see some brother or sister in need and have the means to do something about it but turn a cold shoulder and do nothing, what happens to God's love? It disappears. And you made it disappear. (1 John 3:17 MSG)

If you are feeling like your heart has turned cold, I challenge you to ask God for ways for you to open it back up. It could be as simple as encouraging or blessing someone who has cursed or discounted you in the past. Make eye contact when you see someone hurting. Ask them, "How can I help?" Decide what you can do and follow through with what you say. If they ask for something you cannot help them with, connect them with someone who can. These solutions usually happen in community.

OUT OF REACH

Then there is the unreal and often highly agitated world of social media. These are the people who hear and see what you show them, but your lives will never intersect. This realm requires healthy boundaries and rules of engagement if you are to save your emotional energy. If you read a post and don't agree with what it is saying, don't get worked up. Don't receive the pressure to judge or give an opinion. You don't have to like every post. You don't have to get into an argument. We will never agree with everything that everyone says, and that's okay. I don't even agree with all the things I've said in the past! What's not okay is getting entangled emotionally when someone says something you don't agree with, then getting in strife. This steals your time and energy from what truly matters.

I am constantly asked if the cruel things people say to me or about me on social media affect me. I am not heartless. Of course their words might sting, but I refuse to give strangers that much power over my life. I have been blessed to be surrounded by people who truly care about me. They are invited to wound me with truth so that I can grow and exemplify a greater measure of God's love.

There are amazing things to learn and discover on social media. It can be a great tool of communication on so many levels. Other times, the fights that happen on it are emotional distractions that should be ignored. You don't have to answer everyone who shouts at you. You don't have to answer people who aren't really looking for answers. Sometimes trolls or angry people are just looking for people they can abuse. In this case, answering them will add fuel to the wrong fire and possibly keep them from having meaningful conversations with the real people in their world. Proverbs 18:2 warns us, "A fool takes no pleasure in understanding, but only in expressing his opinion."

Don't get caught in their foolishness; use your time to pursue the wisdom found in understanding. Loving everyone does not mean granting everyone equal access to your life. It is impossible to have the same level of intimacy with everyone. If you are married, your husband deserves more attention than your screen. Your children have the right to eye contact and face-to-face uninterrupted conversations with you.

Even Jesus had different levels of relational intimacy with his disciples. By all accounts, he was the closest with John. He shared conversations with John that the others only heard about afterward. We see the designation of "the disciple Jesus loved" four times in the New Testament. Jesus loved all his disciples, but that does not mean the individual relationships looked the same.

I guarantee that in my time of prayer today, I heard something different than you did. Why? We are not the same person, nor do we have the same challenges. God loves and speaks to each of his daughters uniquely. There were seasons in my life when my relationship with Jesus was more transactional when he wanted it to be transformational. He was as involved as I would let him be at the time.

We've all poured into people who later pulled away. But here is the good news: those seeds are never lost. We sow and God gives the increase. Sometimes your words will meet them in a later season when they are ready to hear them. Don't withdraw or go inward and imagine that there is something wrong with you. Let's be bigger women than that.

Learn from me; don't allow a thousand days to pass before you reach out. There are redemptive seeds within every misunderstanding when we make reconciliation the goal. Rather than continue to allow confusion to cloud your vantage, be courageous enough to confront for the sake of peace. Look for those opportunities, and the next time you experience a "suddenly" when you are at the altar, consider it an invitation to move toward restoration. I'll bet there is someone out there just waiting for your call.

Godmother Conversation Starters

Is there a confusing dynamic or conversation that you've been avoiding?

Was there a "suddenly" when you were in prayer that you pushed aside?

What can you do today to change that?

What are some boundaries that you need to put in place so that your emotional energy isn't depleted by strangers?

Thirteen

How to Be One

There's no way to be a perfect mother and a million ways to be a good one.

—Jill Churchill

Let's not strive for the impossible and miss opportunities for growth. When it comes to being any type of a mother, perfection quickly morphs into the enemy of good. It's time to stop being so hard on ourselves! We can have perfect love for others, but it doesn't mean we will have a perfect relationship. The pursuit of "perfect" is an unreasonable standard that frustrates rather than inspires. Our goal should be growth rather than the improbable. The good news is, you can be the perfect godmother for a given situation. To be this, God factors in our flaws along with our strengths.

One of the many ways to be a good mother is to be a woke one! This is a mama who is paying attention. She is awake and aware.

Deborah was an extraordinary woman who served Israel as both judge and prophetess when the nation was at one of its lowest points. Deborah's predecessor was Ehud. He freed Israel from Moabite oppression, turned the people from idol worship, reestablished the nation's borders, and judged the nation for eighty years. With his death, the people returned to their former evil practices. Judges 4 opens with,

> And the people of Israel again did what was evil in the sight of the LORD after Ehud died. (v. 1)

After eight decades of peace, perhaps they forgot what difficulty looked like. In a protracted time of security, it is easy for a nation to forget its source. When Israel turned away from God, he rectified the situation by turning them over to one of their enemies.

> And the LORD sold them into the hand of Jabin king of Canaan, who reigned in Hazor. The commander of his army was Sisera, who lived in Harosheth-hagoyim. Then the people of Israel cried out to the LORD for help, for he had 900 chariots of iron and he oppressed the people of Israel cruelly for twenty years. (Judg. 4:2–3)

The eighty years of peace were followed by two decades of cruel oppression. Israel was devastated, disheartened, discouraged, and disengaged.

This was the condition of her people when Deborah became their prophetess judge. Spiritually, her people had lost their way. A few commentaries mention how demoralizing it must have been for their patriarchal culture to have a woman as their leader (though nothing in the passage alludes to this).

Desperate times call for desperate measures, and sometimes a godmother is what is needed.

It is not clear how a woman came to this position. It could be that it was the only type of leadership that their oppressor allowed. Perhaps Israel's male leadership was killed, and the few who remained were in hiding, discouraged, or displaced. Whatever the cause, Deborah found herself holding dual positions of both legal and spiritual governance.

> Now Deborah, a prophetess, the wife of Lappidoth, was judging Israel at that time. She used to sit under the palm of Deborah between Ramah and Bethel in the hill country of Ephraim, and the people of Israel came up to her for judgment. (Judg. 4:4–5)

Deborah held court under a palm tree between two desolate cities filled with hurting and hopeless people. Israel's trade routes had been cut off, and the people refused to work the surrounding fields for fear of being attacked by their oppressors. For two decades, not only were things bad for Israel they were bad in Israel. The nation was oppressed without and divided within. Day in and day out, Deborah sat and listened to mediate their arguments and disputes.

Then something happened.

She realized nothing changes while we simply sit and judge. Change requires action, and action involves engagement and risk. It is so much easier to observe than it is to do. It was time to confront the enemy. I wonder if she was tired of watching her people cower in fear and squabble among one another.

Change requires action, and action involves engagement and risk.

The following verse captures Deborah's response to the need of her nation:

> Village life ceased, it ceased in Israel, Until I, Deborah, arose,
> Arose a mother in Israel. (Judg. 5:7 NKJV)

Fear had completely shut down life in their communities. The people were afraid to dream, afraid to live, and afraid to hope. Enough was enough; rather than sit as a judge, the prophetess Deborah rose to mother her nation. It is one thing to judge and quite another to mother. Mothers have a God-given fierceness when it comes to their children. Another version reads,

> Warriors were scarce; they were scarce in Israel,
> until you arose, Deborah, until you arose as a
> motherly protector in Israel. (Judg. 5:7 NET)

I like to imagine that godmother is another way of saying motherly protector. Long periods of peace do not give birth to warriors. It would seem that when mothers awake, the warriors arise. The NCV reads,

> There were no warriors in Israel
> until I, Deborah, arose,
> until I arose to be a mother to Israel. (Judg. 5:7)

And possibly my favorite version, just for fun . . .

> Warriors became fat and sloppy,
> no fight left in them.
> Then you, Deborah, rose up;
> you got up, a mother in Israel. (Judg. 5:7 MSG)

Whether there were no warriors or just a few fat ones, everything changed when Deborah arose as a mother. Mothers fight for their sons and daughters. Deborah wasn't trying to build a kingdom. After being both a judge and a prophetess for two decades, she recognized that Israel needed a mother. She went into action:

> She sent and summoned Barak the son of Abinoam from Kedesh-naphtali and said to him, "Has not the LORD, the God of Israel, commanded you, 'Go, gather your men at Mount Tabor, taking 10,000 from the people of Naphtali and the people of Zebulun.'" (Judg. 4:6)

Barak pushed back and refused to confront the enemy unless accompanied by Deborah. Scripture is unclear whether he was afraid or just in need of her support. Rather than argue, Deborah lent him her strength. There is an important lesson for all of us in her response. True leaders lend strength rather than pull rank. At the end of the day, it is about getting the job done rather than doing it alone. Mothers understand that moving a child from one place to another can be as simple as walking with them.

True leaders lend strength rather than pull rank.

The enemy is confronted, the evil leader comes to a bad end at the hands of another woman. It's all pretty intense in chapter 4; then there is a retelling of Israel's victory in the form of a prophetic song in chapter 5. In these verses, we discover that some confrontations on earth are reflected in the realms of heaven. Judges 5:20–21 lends us a window into what was happening in the spirit realm:

From the heavens the stars fought,
    from their courses they fought against Sisera.
The river Kishon swept them away,
    the age-old river, the river Kishon.
    March on, my soul; be strong! (NIV)

When mothers awake, the children of Most High God arise! As we sing our way into battle, the very stars are fighting on our behalf! This is beyond exciting! Few of us hold the position of judges and prophetesses. Don't imagine these type of positions are what is required for us to begin. To begin all you need to have is the heart of a mother.

WARRIOR MOTHERS

To be a mother is to be a warrior. We fight for life. True mothers want more for their children than what they experienced. My prayer is that where I've known oppression, my children will know freedom and that my failures will serve to position them for success. Conversely, our mother's heart hurts when we see the youth stray. Jesus expressed the sentiments of a mother's heart for her children.

O Jerusalem, Jerusalem, the city that kills the prophets and stones those who are sent to it! How often would I have gathered your children together as a hen gathers her brood under her wings, and you were not willing! (Luke 13:34)

Mothers protect. I believe God is inviting us to be godmothers who are mother protectors. When we arise, men, women, and children are protected. Goddaughters and godmothers, look around. What do you see?

Are there gaps?

Do you see warriors or infighting?

Are we fighting about what really matters?

Are we neglecting what really does?

Is it important that everyone knows what we are against?

Rather than give opinions, it's time to live the truth in love.

Do you see the sons and daughters?

Have they lost hope and forgotten their royal name?

Are our villages vibrant with life?

Are the gates of our lives open or closed in fear?

What ground are we afraid to plant?

What lost territory are we afraid to take back?

Who is at risk if we do not find ways to close these breaches?

Mothers see the problem and move quickly toward a solution.

Having a mother's heart begins with blessing others in the very areas we once felt cursed. Being a mother is a willingness to pour out what was never poured into us. It is when we leave behind the titles of judge and prophet and open our arms to the very ones that may reject us. It is as simple as offering to walk alongside them.

> *Having a mother's heart begins with blessing others in the very areas we once felt cursed.*

I wish we could sit together for even ten minutes so I could better convey the urgency and privilege of this godmother mandate. As we sipped whipped cream–topped espresso, I would spread out before you the more than six hundred questions I've received from daughters who ranged from young single women to new brides to young mothers, ministers, and lonely, discouraged older women.

If espresso is not your thing, then you could come by later and I'd make you pasta. Side by side, we would review their earnest questions that run the gauntlet from marriage to ministry. Some inquiries are easy: What do you think about tattoos? I'm fine with tattoos; I have one myself. Other questions are much harder and probe deeper. Some have caused me to blink back tears. Some I don't have answers for. This is where you come into the picture. They need you. I need you.

There are goddaughters who want to hear what you have learned. They want to be seen as well as shown. They want to hear your regrets and share your joy. They need someone who reminds them that motherhood is both exhausting and amazing. There are single mothers who need to hear that they are heroes who should be helped by us in every way we find ourselves capable of. There are single daughters who need to hear that marriage isn't the answer to everything. Divorced women who find themselves cruelly cast off or suddenly alone. All of these need older women who have learned how to navigate the tides of time so they won't miss the strength of their current season. They need someone safe to help them dream as well as navigate the pain of betrayal.

You may be thinking, *Wait a minute, I am not old!* Friend, you don't have to be old; you just have to be an old soul. We have amazing friends who pastor in Singapore, and in their church, *everyone* is positioned to pour into *someone* younger . . . fifteen-year-olds are pouring into twelve-year-olds. This means we are all godmothers as much as we are goddaughters.

A GODMOTHER'S ASSIGNMENT

Goddaughters grow in godliness when there is less of us and more of Christ. The benefit of your length of days is that you've had a bit more time to experience God's faithfulness. In the same way, goddaughters don't need us to be fascinating, cool, or even original. They simply need us to be faithful. His interaction in our story is glorious enough to act as a guide for others.

> *Faithful godmothers lift the name of Jesus, the words of Jesus, and the ways of Jesus over and above their own.*

Faithful godmothers lift the name of Jesus, the words of Jesus, and the ways of Jesus over and above their own.

Like all the older women who profess Christ, I am charged with a very special assignment that is hidden within Paul's letter to Titus.

> Your duty is to teach them to embrace a lifestyle that is consistent with sound doctrine. Lead the male elders into disciplined lives full of dignity and self-control. Urge them to have a solid faith, generous love, and patient endurance. (Titus 2:1–2 TPT)

It is so confusing when lifestyle contradicts beliefs. When Titus was written, there were no Bibles; they had living examples. Crete had heard the gospel; now it was time to live it. The believers were about to become disciples. This shift would require elders or godparents. People hear what we say but follow what we model. Titus was Paul's son in the faith. Titus knew the gospel because he watched Paul live the gospel. Next, Paul addressed how the women should be involved.

Likewise with the female elders [or older women], lead them into lives free from gossip and drunkenness and to be teachers of beautiful things [the Greek reads *good things*]. This will enable them to teach the younger women to love their husbands, to love their children, and to be self-controlled and pure, taking care of their household and being devoted to their husbands. By doing these things the word of God will not be discredited. (Titus 2:3–5 TPT)

Just as with the men, Paul wanted the women to model behavior consistent with those who profess to follow Christ. The older and younger women were together on this learning journey. There was a lot said in these five verses that I'd like to bring forward.

Right away we notice that *age was honored*. The older women were the ones who were best equipped to teach the younger. Please hear me, my older sisters: this is an invitation for you to embrace your age and the strength that comes with this stage of life. The best way we can do this is to honor God in all that we do.

Next, godmothers are charged to *live free from gossip*. I interpret this as don't read it, don't speak it, don't repeat it, don't listen to it. Why? Is gossip really so destructive? Very loosely paraphrasing James, gossip is like breathing fire. It kills what once was healthy and destroys what once was whole. We are empowered to release the blessings that turn the unfavorable circumstances around to favorable. Let's not adopt the role of an accuser and curse the very ones God desires to bless. Our words reveal our maturity.

We all fail in many areas, but especially with our words. Yet if we're able to bridle the words we say we are powerful enough to control ourselves in every way, and that means our character is mature and fully developed. (James 3:2 TPT)

Our level of self-control will be revealed in our speech. If I find I am in a sorry state, and I am concerned I will not be able to control what comes out of my mouth, I put myself in time-out until I can. *Godmothers must avoid all forms of gossip.*

Rather than repeat rumors, let's declare the incorruptible Word. Rather than repeat tales that might cause division, let's use our words to lift others. If we've repeated things that should have remained in silence, then it is time to simply stop. There are so many things I do not understand or agree with, but that does not mean that I have to give my opinion to the masses.

> Fire goes out without wood,
>   and quarrels disappear when gossip stops.
>   (Prov. 26:20 NLT)

If it's not your fire, stop adding wood to it. Don't stoke the flame, don't blow on it. Starve the flame, and it will burn itself out.

Don't drink to the point of drunkenness. It dulls your senses and causes you to miss what is important. And then, of course, you'll run the risk of saying or doing something you'll regret later.

Godmothers are empowered with the purpose of teaching. Let's not just read the Word of God; let's live it. This enables us to teach the younger women the good and worthy pursuits of life and position them to discover what is genuinely beautiful.

Love requires learning. We are not born knowing how to love our husbands or even our children. Building a healthy marriage and family involves work. Love does not mean enabling your husband or spoiling your children. Love naturally causes growth. John and I have grown in love even as our love has grown. People grow when they are loved. No matter what our marriage or mothering story was, we can help the young marriages and families around us grow in love and strength. Each year is another chance to write a new chapter. Don't be afraid to open your life when it comes to marriage and children. Show them how to raise their children by sharing the things you did well and your mistakes.

Wisdom and virtue should be our pursuit. If you're an older woman, don't allow idleness or the pursuit of pleasure to distract you. This can be your most rewarding season of life if you don't devolve into a critic. This world has more than enough critics and detractors; what it needs is mamas who model support. If you are wondering how to do this, why not make kindness your king?

> When she speaks she has something worthwhile to say,
> and she always says it kindly. (Prov. 31:26 MSG)

Sweet one, I know you are wise enough to know it is not just what we say but how we say it. Let's not pretend we are tone deaf. We all hear so much better when kindness is present. People can even hear hard things when they are said in kindness.

> A single act of kindness throws out roots in all directions, and
> the roots spring up and make new trees.
>
> Amelia Earhart

You never know what grows in response to your seeds of kindness. But be assured; something is growing. Our world is growing increasingly unkind and cold, which means there is a desperate need for kind godmothers. Remember, kindness can act like magic and works the most powerfully on the least deserving.

I found the "taking care of their household" part in Titus 2 a bit frustrating until I discovered that *housekeeping is far more than housework.*

> She keeps an eye on everyone in her household,
>   and keeps them all busy and productive.
>   (Prov. 31:27 MSG)

You are not the maid! This verse in Proverbs describes a mother who is doing far more than cleaning up after her family. It describes a mother who is discipling and developing everyone under her care. I want more for my children. This means I want them to grow more rather than get more. It looks different in a marriage than it does with children, but I want to foster the same dynamic of growth in my husband.

I've discovered nurture does better than nagging. If you are married, be devoted to your husband. Be careful not to undermine or dishonor one another in word or deed. It is not easy, but it is worth it. Making one another look bad will never make either

You never know what grows in response to your seeds of kindness. But be assured; something is growing.

of you look good. This has been a hard one for John and me. We both feel things very strongly, and each day is another opportunity for growth. That's the tricky part about being one. When we lash out at one another, we injure ourselves. When I see newlyweds, I tell them it will only keep getting better. Time, trials, children, and shared experiences only serve to enrich your life.

Let's embrace our years (even if some see you as a youth) and all the lessons we've learned and refuse to adopt our culture's worship of youth and frivolity. If you're a younger woman, this means you have lots to look forward to. If you are an older woman like me, it means that you are being watched. Lead by example; hiding or opting out is not an option.

GODMOTHERS IN WHAT WE DO

> When we Christians behave badly, or fail to behave well, we are making Christianity unbelievable to the outside world.
>
> C. S. Lewis[1]

Let's all be part of changing this trend. Let's behave wisely and kindly. Let's stop sitting and judging everyone else's bad behavior and make the time to reflect on our own.

The bottom line of all this instruction is that our lives should not contradict the truth we profess. The choices that we make, both in public and in private, should not confuse the issue of what it looks like to be Christ's. You don't need a doctorate in theology to build a beautiful life.

Here is but a sample of some of the good that women are entrusted to do:

Loving their neighbor. Loving their husband. Loving their children. Loving the orphan. Loving friends. Sharing wisdom. Training others. Learning. Practicing kindness. Being generous. Serving in secret or publicly. Sacrificing. Preaching the gospel. Working. Making your home a haven for family and friends.

Making homes a possibility for others. And loving God is what makes all these beautiful things possible.

There has never been a greater need for all of the above, and yet there has never been more resistance to these concepts. We have a massive gap between lifestyle and the words of life. As I prepared to write this chapter, I looked back over what I'd written on the topic more than a decade ago in my book *Nurture*. The need was great then and is desperate now. The gap has left future generations vulnerable.

> Above all, set yourself apart as a model of a life nobly lived. With dignity, demonstrate integrity in all that you teach. Bring a clear, wholesome message that cannot be condemned, and then your critics will be embarrassed, with nothing bad to say about us. (Titus 2:7–8 TPT)

Paul is telling Titus to make his example of a Christ-filled life the highest priority. What does it mean to behave nobly? Among other things, it means to be an example of what is good, gracious, kind, virtuous, just, moral, polite, and self-sacrificing. Living nobly is about living in a way that honors others rather than ourselves. Living nobly says I belong to an ever-expanding family of nobility that I want you to be part of. Living nobly is how we respond to others, and it is completely independent of our income. We are noble because of our heavenly birthright, utterly independent of our earthly inheritance.

We are noble because of our heavenly birthright, utterly independent of our earthly inheritance.

We live in a day that is more likely to celebrate the ignoble, shameful, immoral, and poor example. There is a lot of criticism levied at anything that hints of purity and wholesomeness. When this happens, bless those who criticize and move on. The ones who want to hear what you have to say will seem quieter than those who don't . . . say and live it anyway. Paul continues his letter to Titus with instructions of how to further train the believers:

> And remind them to never tear down anyone with their words or quarrel, but instead be considerate, humble, and courteous to everyone. For it wasn't that long ago that we behaved foolishly in our stubborn disobedience. We were easily led astray as slaves to worldly passions and pleasures. We wasted our lives in doing evil, and with hateful jealousy we hated others. (Titus 3:1–3 TPT)

Paul is in essence saying, "Remember when you were messed up, and you messed up?" Our Lord dealt gently with us when we didn't know better; let's deal gently with those who are learning or don't know better. Now that we know just how powerful our words are, let's be wise with how we use words with our children, our husband, and our friends. The greater our potential for influence, the less freedom we have to misuse it.

We are ambassadors of another kingdom rather than celebrities of our own. So how do we begin? Let's start with this: godmothers aren't perfect. No pressure. Just begin where you are. It doesn't matter how messy your life is, there is something in it that others need.

Be Aware

Pray and ask God the Father to open your eyes to see your potential goddaughters, wherever they may be. Then watch in faith for them. They are all around us. Here is a secret: god-daughters hide in plain sight, hoping someone sees them. Many are afraid of being rejected if they ask for help, so they suffer in silence. Others think asking for help is a sign of weakness. Assure them it is not. Asking for help is not weakness; it's wisdom.

Acknowledge

When you see goddaughters, respond to them. It can be as simple as a smile or a nod. It costs you nothing to greet some-one. Recently I was in the ladies' room with one of my grand-daughters, and I noticed a young woman looking our way. I wasn't sure if she was responding to my interaction with my granddaughter or to me directly. I smiled. It wasn't long before she came up to me. She shared how my messages and the books had touched her life, and right there and then, we hugged in the women's restroom. Easy. But what if I had looked away or sent the message that I couldn't be bothered? Without knowing it, I'd be undermining the seeds I'd sown in her life.

Be Engaged

Ask "How can I help?" Some will respond to your invita-tion; others will not. That's okay; you are not responsible for their response. You're responsible to simply offer. Some will be ready to hear from you; others may come back to you in another season. And sometimes the best way to connect is to ask them for help. There were a number of girls I mentored by inviting them into my world, and they did life alongside me. I still hear from them and how they applied what they learned with the children they had.

Be Available

Not all the time. I'm not asking you to allow anyone to monopolize your life, but I am asking you to set time aside so that you can be available to be with them. I have goddaughters I rarely see in person, but we speak on the phone, text, and, whenever we can, connect in person.

Be Authentic

Don't say one thing and live another. That's fake. Authentic means faithful, reliable, honest, and genuine. Goddaughters are not looking for us to be more than we are; they need us to be more than they are. I heard one young female minister say it this way: "We don't need the older women to be cool, because you're not cool; we need you to be wise and godly." Let's switch some things around and make it cool to be wise and godly!

Be Active

Be about your Father's business. Get involved with something you're passionate about. Another term for active is *in force*. Virtuous women are a force for good. Be engaged on an interactive level. Liking a photo engages with someone's social platform, which is good, but picking up the phone and calling someone engages them. Open your home to teach something—anything—that you're passionate about! It doesn't have to be a Bible study; why not share something you love? You could share on investing, marriage, gardening, or friendship. Think of something you'd be confident sharing, and simply host daughters. Who knows, maybe I will do a pesto class simply because I love it!

Be an Advocate

We all need people in our lives who encourage us, because discouragement has reached epidemic levels. Part of encouraging others is moving their feet in the right direction. It is confronting what is off course while celebrating what is on track. This one can be tricky. You can be an advocate for the person without endorsing everything they do.

We live in a day when many people are looking for gaps rather than for ways to close them. Words are spun, motives are twisted, people are afraid to speak up on behalf of others for fear that the gap experts will turn on them. This is not living. This is a sign that village life has ceased and the warriors are gone. Here is what I want godmothers to be known for:

> You'll use the old rubble of past lives to build anew,
>> rebuild the foundations from out of your past.
> You'll be known as those who can fix anything,
>> restore old ruins, rebuild and renovate,
>> make the community livable again.
>> (Isa. 58:12 MSG)

Everywhere we look, we see war and anger. Everyone wants you to choose sides. And yet the words of Jesus speak of better things. He tells us that amid all the strife there will be those who make peace.

> Blessed are the peacemakers: for they shall be called the children of God. (Matt. 5:9 KJV)

It is time for us to live in such a way that this could be said of us. That someone could look at me, you, or the collective us and whisper, "Did you see that? Did you hear her? Did you feel that? There goes a child of God."

The Message translation says it this way: "You're blessed when you can show people how to cooperate instead of compete or fight. That's when you discover who you really are, and your place in God's family" (Matt. 5:9 MSG).

Do you hear this?

We discover who we really are by helping others. We discover our place in God's family by making peace. We need godmothers and godfathers to help the sons and daughters learn how to work together rather than compete and fight. As we do this for them, we discover our purpose and place.

Tonight, I host a birthday dinner for one of my sons. We are in a new house and a new season. Our home is poised as a place to make new memories. The dining table from our old house is upstairs waiting to be used later as a game table. Our new table is long, and for the first time all of the adults will fit comfortably. I've already set it. I want everyone to know that even though the table is new, they will always have a place at it. I hope it says that they are watched for, welcome, and expected. There is something so powerful about knowing you are always included.

It isn't long before laughter fills the air. One granddaughter rides upside down on the back of an uncle who claims to have lost her. Tonight's dinner is simple: hamburgers, Italian soda, grilled vegetables, salad, and three different flavors of chips. The table overflows with an assortment of sliced white cheddar, sauerkraut, pickles, two ketchups, and three different mustards.

The sliding glass door stays open as we move outside to catch the warmth of fading sunshine.

The sunset is spectacular. The sky bursts into fiery reds and corals as the autumn sun dips below the mountain range. Before the temperature drops too low, we gather around the firepit to laugh, dream, and roast marshmallows.

Peace is not always quiet.

Peace is not everything in its place.

Peace is not when everything is perfect.

Peace is found when we know where to place our trust.

Peace can be a table full of food and a house full of laughter.

Peace can be a quiet day of fasting in solitude.

Peace wraps us like a blanket in seasons of deep grief and pain.

Peace warms our lives like sunshine in seasons of joy.

Peace is an early morning sunrise.

Peace is a glorious sunset with a dog barking.

Peace is not found in compromise.

Peace is a promise that requires work.

Peacemakers are not always passive.

Peace always finds its way to those who are brave enough to make it.

"Blessed are the peacemakers: for they shall be called the children of God," and what more could a godmother want?

Beautiful brave goddaughters and godmothers, now is the time for you to do. Walk forward wisely and bravely trusting that God will weave us together in wonder.

Acknowledgments

I would be remiss if I didn't take this space to thank those who played a part in making this book possible.

Andrea, you've believed in this project from the very start. Thank you for your consistent support and wise editorial input. It was truly invaluable.

Team Revell, you are a dream to work with. I am thankful for our relational partnership.

Esther, thank you for making these connections happen.

A special thanks to our Messenger International team, who supported me in prayer and sacrificed time with me to see this project move forward.

And a final word of thanks to my family. You are the ones who grow in ways no one else will ever know. I love being related to each of you.

My husband John: after nearly four decades, you still make me laugh.

To my four sons: Addison, Austin, Alec, and Arden, I am so honored to simply be your mother. There is nothing and no one I am prouder of.

To my three daughters in love: Julianna, Jessica, and Christian, I am inspired by the beautiful way each of you lives and loves.

To my four grands: Asher, Sophia, Lizzy, and August. You cause my heart to sing.

Notes

Chapter One Why You Need One

1. *Merriam-Webster*, s.v. "gap (n.)," https://www.merriam-webster.com /dictionary/gap.

Chapter Two Begin with What You Know

1. C. S. Lewis, *Letters to Malcolm, Chiefly on Prayer* (New York: Harper-Collins, 1964), 75.
2. L. M. Montgomery, *Anne of Green Gables* (Boston: LC Page & Co., 1908).

Chapter Three Ask for What You Need

1. George Sweeting, *Who Said That?* (Chicago: Moody Publishers, 1995), "Action" section, https://books.google.com/books?id=7mn8AwAAQBAJ&pg.
2. George Mueller, *Answers to Prayer* (Chicago: Moody Publishers, 1984).
3. *Merriam-Webster*, s.v. "abide (v.)," https://www.merriam-webster.com /dictionary/abide.

Chapter Four When Healing Is What You Need

1. N. T. Wright, *Matthew for Everyone, Part 1, Chapters 1–15* (Louisville: Presbyterian Publishing Corporation, 2004), 200.

Chapter Six Write Your Way Forward

1. Lee Iacocca with William Novak, *Iacocca: An Autobiography* (New York: Bantam, 1986), 50.
2. *Merriam-Webster*, s.v. "arc (n.)," https://www.merriam-webster.com /dictionary/arc.
3. *Merriam-Webster*, s.v. "arc (n.)."

4. Adrienne LaFrance, "The Six Main Arcs in Storytelling, as Identified by an A.I.," *Atlantic*, July 12, 2016, https://www.theatlantic.com/technology /archive/2016/07/the-six-main-arcs-in-storytelling-identified-by-a-computer /490733/.

Chapter Seven Focus Is Your Superpower

1. https://www.brainyquote.com/quotes/jacqueline_leo_547986.
2. https://www.goodreads.com/quotes/386121-paper-is-to-write-things -down-that-we-need-to.
3. N. T. Wright, *Surprised by Scripture* (New York: HarperOne, 2014), 70.

Chapter Eight The Balancing Act

1. C. S. Lewis, *The Four Loves* (New York: Harcourt Brace, 1960), 120.

Chapter Nine When Our Fairy Tales Go Awry

1. "Cinderella Around the World," http://www.edenvalleyenterprises.org /blhrc/educational/cindtour/world.html.
2. LaFrance, "The Six Main Arcs in Storytelling."
3. J. R. R. Tolkien, *The Tolkien Reader* (Logan, IA: Perfection Learning, 1986), 68–69.
4. Sarah Ban Breathnach, *Simple Abundance* (New York: Grand Central, 1995), February 16 entry.
5. C. S. Lewis, *The Screwtape Letters* (New York, HarperCollins, 1961).
6. United States Census Bureau, "America's Families and Living Arrange-ments: 2018," Table FG10, Family Groups: 2018, https://www.census.gov /data/tables/2018/demo/families/cps-2018.html.
7. K. M. O'Connor, "Jeremiah," in *Women's Bible Commentary*, rev. and updated, eds. C. A. Newsom, J. E. Lapsley, and S. H. Ringe (Louisville: West-minster John Knox Press, 2012), 276.

Chapter Ten The Gender Gap

1. "How Many Species on Earth?," California Academy of Sciences, August 24, 2011, https://www.calacademy.org/explore-science/how-many -species-on-earth.
2. Roger Highfield, "Bone Marrow Cell Study Adds to Clone Campaign," *Telegraph*, May 4, 2001, https://www.telegraph.co.uk/news/worldnews/north america/usa/1329123/Bone-marrow-cell-study-adds-to-clone-campaign.html.
3. Lisa Bevere, *Fight Like a Girl* (New York: FaithWords, 2006), 26–27.
4. Bob Utley, *How It All Began: Genesis 1–11, Vol. 1A* (Marshall, TX: Bible Lessons International, 2001), 49.
5. Kara Maria Ananda, "7 Wonders of the Womb," Wellness Blessing, https://wellnessblessing.com/blog/wonders-of-the-womb.

6. Philip Barton Payne, *Man and Woman, One in Christ: An Exegetical and Theological Study of Paul's Letters* (Grand Rapids: Zondervan, 2015), ch. 12.

7. Wright, *Surprised by Scripture*, 76.

8. Payne, *Man and Woman, One in Christ*, ch. 12.

9. N. T. Wright, *Paul for Everyone: The Pastoral Letters, 1 and 2 Timothy and Titus* (London: Society for Promoting Christian Knowledge, 2004), 21–22.

10. Wright, *Paul for Everyone: 1 and 2 Timothy and Titus*, 21–26.

Chapter Eleven When Godmothers and Goddaughters Connect

1. Lisa Bevere, *Without Rival* (Grand Rapids: Revell, 2016), 181.

2. M. R. De Haan, *The Romance of Redemption: Studies in the Book of Ruth* (Grand Rapids: Kregel, 1996), 18.

Chapter Twelve When Godmothers and Goddaughters Collide

1. Eugene H. Peterson, *Five Smooth Stones for Pastoral Work* (Grand Rapids: Eerdmans, 1980), 54.

2. Social media post used by permission.

Chapter Thirteen How to Be One

1. C. S. Lewis, *Mere Christianity* (New York: HarperCollins, 2001), 208.

Lisa Bevere has spent nearly three decades empowering women of all ages to find their identity and purpose. She is a *New York Times* bestselling author and internationally known speaker. Her previous books, which include *Fight Like a Girl, Lioness Arising, Girls with Swords, Without Rival,* and *Adamant,* are in the hands of millions worldwide. Lisa and her husband, John, are the founders of Messenger International, an organization committed to developing uncompromising followers of Christ who transform their world. Learn more at www.lisabevere.com.

TRUTH has a name.

Theologically deep yet intimately accessible.
Adamant will be an anchor for your soul in a
raging sea of opinions, giving you a clear sense
of direction in a wandering world.

BOOKS BY LISA

Adamant*

Without Rival*

Be Angry but Don't Blow It!

Fight Like a Girl*

Girls with Swords*

It's Not How You Look, It's What You See

Lioness Arising*

Kissed the Girls and Made Them Cry*

Nurture*

Out of Control and Loving It!

The True Measure of a Woman

You Are Not What You Weigh

*Available in study format

Messenger International exists to develop uncompromising followers of Christ who transform our world.

Call: **1-800-648-1477**

Visit us online at: **MessengerInternational.org**

STAY CONNECTED WITH LISA!

LisaBevere.com

And be sure to TUNE IN to Lisa's podcast

The Godmother,

available on iTunes, Spotify, or wherever
you get your podcasts.